Love Letters of Great Men and Women

Edited by Ursula Doyle

PAN BOOKS

Love Letters of Great Men was first published in 2008 by Macmillan;
Love Letters of Great Women was first published in 2009, also by Macmillan.

First published together in paperback as
Love Letters of Great Men and Women 2010 by Pan Books
an imprint of Pan Macmillan, a division of Macmillan Publishers Limited
Pan Macmillan, 20 New Wharf Road, London N1 9RR
Basingstoke and Oxford
Associated companies throughout the world
www.panmacmillan.com

ISBN: 978-0-330-51513-9

A CIP catalogue record for this book is available from
the British Library.

Printed by CPI Mackays, Chatham ME5 8TD

Visit **www.panmacmillan.com** to read more about all our books
and to buy them. You will also find features, author interviews and
news of any author events, and you can sign up for e-newsletters
so that you're always first to hear about our new releases.

Contents

Love Letters of Great Men

Love Letters of Great Women

Love Letters
of Great Men

Introduction

The commonly held view these days is that people don't write love letters any more, and that email and text messaging are death to romance. And it does seem unlikely that even the most impassioned lover would today claim, as the playwright Congreve does, that 'nothing but you can lay hold of my mind, and that can lay hold of nothing but you'; then again, Congreve was a literary genius. But Nelson most definitely was not, and even he came up with the stirring formulation, to Lady Hamilton, 'Nelson's Alpha and Omega is Emma!' Perhaps people have grown less romantic and more cynical. Or perhaps people were less self-conscious than we are today; certainly, irony, the presiding spirit of our age, has almost no place in this collection.

So, while reading all these love letters, and finding out the stories behind them, it was tempting to think that we modern barbarians have lost faith, both in love itself and in the art of its expression. But in fact, for the most part, it wasn't the elegantly worked, impassioned declarations that I found most touching in the letters that follow, or rather, not those alone; it was when they bumped up against more prosaic concerns, like the unreliability of the postal service, or the need for clean linen, or the sending of regards to the beloved's mother, or a description of a dream, that the letters suddenly came alive somehow, and their writers seemed more human. It could be argued that the flowery declarations were more for show (and, in some cases, posterity) than the genuine expression of genuine feeling – that they grew from convention rather than conviction. And there is a case for calling this book, 'Great Men: Going On About Themselves Since AD 61' – certainly some of those here would have benefited from being taken aside and gently told: it's not All About You.

But to claim that a text message saying IN PUB FTBL XTR TIME BACK LATR XX is more genuine, and therefore romantic, than a declaration such as Byron's that 'I more than love you and cannot cease to love you' is obviously nonsense. So while it is to be hoped that this collection entertains, moves and sometimes amuses its readers, it might also serve to remind today's Great Men that literary genius is not a requirement for a heartfelt letter – or text message, or email – of love.

Ursula Doyle, London, 2008

John Donne
Anne Donne
Un-done

*John Donne writing from Fleet Prison to his wife
after their secret wedding, December 1601*

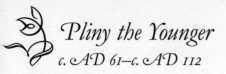

Pliny the Younger
c. AD 61–c. AD 112

Pliny the Younger (Gaius Plinius Caecilius Secundus) was the son of a landowner in northern Italy. After the death of his father, he was brought up by his uncle, Pliny the Elder, the author of a famous encyclopaedia on natural history. In AD 79, Pliny the Elder was killed during the eruption of Vesuvius.

Pliny had a career in law and government, first as a consul, and then as governor of a Roman province. He left behind ten books of letters: nine to friends and colleagues, the tenth to the emperor Trajan.

To Calpurnia, his wife

You will not believe what a longing for you possesses me. The chief cause of this is my love; and then we have not grown used to be apart. So it comes to pass that I lie awake a great part of the night, thinking of you; and that by day, when the hours return at which I was wont to visit you, my feet take me, as it is so truly said, to your chamber, but not finding you there I return, sick and sad at heart, like an excluded lover. The only time that is free from these torments is when I am being worn out at the bar, and in the suits of my friends. Judge you what must be my life when I find my repose in toil, my solace in wretchedness and anxiety. Farewell.

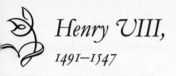

Henry VIII,
1491–1547

Henry VIII first encountered Anne Boleyn in 1526, when he was married to his first wife, Katherine of Aragon. The Roman Catholic Church did not allow divorce, and so Henry, obsessed with Anne, who refused to become his mistress, moved heaven and earth to persuade the Pope to grant him an annulment. The Pope refused, which led to Henry's break with Rome and the establishment of the Church of England with Henry as its Supreme Head (Henry did not have problems with self-esteem: see the kind gift to Anne he mentions in the letter below). The couple were finally married, after seven years of turmoil, in January 1533, and Anne gave birth to her daughter Elizabeth (who became Elizabeth I) that September. In May 1536, Queen Anne was arrested and charged with adultery with several men including her own brother, George, Viscount Rochford. She was found guilty, and beheaded at the Tower of London. On the same day, her marriage to Henry was declared null and void. Eleven days later, Henry married Jane Seymour, the only one of the lucky six wives to bear him a son who survived him, Edward VI.

※ ※ ※

To Anne Boleyn

My Mistress and my Friend:

My heart and I surrender themselves into your hands, and we supplicate to be commended to your good graces, and that by absence your affections may not be diminished to us, for that would be to augment our pain, which would be a great pity, since absence gives enough, and more than I ever thought could be felt. This brings to my mind a fact in astronomy, which is, that the further the poles are from the sun, notwithstanding, the more scorching is the heat. Thus is it with our love; absence has placed distance between us, nevertheless fervor increases – at least on my part. I hope the same from you, assuring you that in my case the anguish of absence is so great that it would be intolerable were it not for the firm hope I have of your indissoluble affection towards me. In order to remind you of it, and because I cannot in person be in your presence, I send you the thing which comes nearest that is possible, that is to say, my picture, and the whole device, which you already know of, set in bracelets, wishing myself in their place when it pleases you. This is from the hand of

Your servant and friend,

H.R.

William Congreve
1670–1729

William Congreve was a celebrated dramatist, best known for his play *The Way of the World*; Arabella Hunt was a musician at Court and a favourite of Queen Mary. Arabella was married in 1680 to one James Howard; she filed for an annulment six months later on the not-unreasonable grounds that James was actually a cross-dressing widow called Amy Poulter. Unsurprisingly, Arabella never married again ('Mrs' was at this time an honorary form of address for a woman out of her teens). Congreve also remained unmarried, but had longstanding love affairs with Anna Bracegirdle, an actress for whom he wrote a number of parts, and Henrietta, Duchess of Marlborough, with whom he had a daughter in 1723.

To Mrs Arabella Hunt

Dear Madam
– Not believe that I love you? You cannot pretend to be so incredulous. If you do not believe my tongue, consult my eyes, consult your own. You will find by yours that they

have charms; by mine that I have a heart which feels them. Recall to mind what happened last night. That at least was a lover's kiss. Its eagerness, its fierceness, its warmth, expressed the god its parent. But oh! Its sweetness, and its melting softness expressed him more. With trembling in my limbs, and fevers in my soul, I ravish'd it. Convulsions, pantings, murmurings shew'd the mighty disorder within me: the mighty disorder increased by it. For those dear lips shot through my heart, and thro' my bleeding vitals, delicious poison, and an avoidless but yet a charming ruin.

What cannot a day produce? The night before I thought myself a happy man, in want of nothing, and in fairest expectation of fortune; approved of by men of wit, and applauded by others. Pleased, nay charmed with my friends, my then dearest friends, sensible of every delicate pleasure, and in their turns possessing all.

But Love, almighty Love, seems in a moment to have removed me to a prodigious distance from every object but you alone. In the midst of crowds I remain in solitude. Nothing but you can lay hold of my mind, and that can lay hold of nothing but you. I appear transported to some foreign desert with you (oh, that I were really thus transported!), where, abundantly supplied with everything, in thee, I might live out an age of uninterrupted ecstasy.

The scene of the world's great stage seems suddenly and sadly chang'd. Unlovely objects are all around me, excepting thee; the charms of all the world appear to be translated to thee. Thus in this sad, but oh, too pleasing state! my soul can fix upon nothing but thee; thee it contemplates, admires, adores, nay depends on, trusts on you alone.

If you and hope forsake it, despair and endless misery attend it.

Richard Steele
1672–1729

Richard Steele was a journalist, writer and politician, who with his friend Joseph Addison founded the *Spectator* magazine. Mary Scurlock was his second wife; he met her at the funeral of his first, and courted her with a single-minded passion. The second letter here, written two weeks before their wedding, is both amusing and touching in Steele's description of himself as a man completely distracted from day-to-day concerns by thoughts of his beloved. Richard and Mary were married in 1707, although their marriage remained secret for some time after that, perhaps for reasons of propriety – this could explain the rather mundane postscript to the third letter below. Their marriage was famously happy, although sometimes tempestuous, and she remained throughout his life his 'dear Prue'. Steele wrote his wife more than four hundred letters both before and during their marriage; she died in 1718.

To Mary Scurlock

Madam,

With what language shall I address my lovely fair to acquaint her with the sentiments of a heart she delights to torture? I have not a minute's quiet out of your sight; and when I am with you, you use me with so much distance, that I am still in a state of absence, heightened with a view of the charms which I am denied to approach. In a word, you must give me either a fan, a mask or a glove you have worn, or I cannot live; otherwise you must expect that I'll kiss your hand, or, when I next sit by you, steal your handkerchief. You yourself are too great a bounty to be secured at once; therefore I must be prepared by degrees, lest the mighty gift distract me with joy.

Dear Miss Scurlock, I am tired with calling you by that name; therefore, say the day in which you will take that of, Madam, your most obedient, most devoted, humble servant,

Rich. Steele

August 1707 (two weeks before their wedding)

Madam,

It is the hardest thing in the world to be in love and yet attend to business. As for me all who speak to me find me out, and I must lock myself up or other people will do it for me.

A gentleman asked me this morning, 'What news from

Lisbon?' and I answered, 'She is exquisitely handsome.' Another desired to know when I had last been at Hampton Court. I replied, 'It will be on Tuesday come se'nniht.' Pr'ythee, allow me at least to kiss your hand before that day, that my mind may be in some composure. O love!

A thousand torments dwell about me!

Yet who would live to live without thee?

Methinks I could write a volume to you; but all the language on earth would fail in saying how much and with what disinterested passion I am ever yours—

Rich. Steele

7 October 1707

My Loved Creature,
I write this only to bid you good-night and assure you of my diligence in the matter I told you of.

You may assure yourself I value you according to your merit which is saying that you have my heart by all the ties of beauty, virtue, good nature and friendship. I find by the progress I have made to-night, that I shall do my business effectually in two days' time. Write me word you are in good humour which will be the highest pleasure to your obliged husband,

Rich. Steele

I shall want some linen from your house tomorrow.

George Farquhar
1676/7–1707

George Farquhar was born in Londonderry, the son of a clergyman, and educated at Trinity College, Dublin. On leaving Trinity, he tried his hand as an actor, but suffered from paralysing stage fright. He made his way to London where his first play, *Love and a Bottle*, was staged in 1698, telling the story of an Irishman newly arrived in the city who is a great success with the ladies. By all accounts, Farquhar was himself both handsome and charming, a wit and a troublemaker.

One night in a tavern, Farquhar heard a young woman named Anne Oldfield reading aloud behind the bar. He was so convinced by her talent that he introduced her to friends in the theatre, and she was taken on as an actress at Drury Lane.

George and Anne's liaison was not long lasting, and in 1703 George married a widow named Margaret Pemell. He had money troubles all his life, and health problems, but even when his difficulties were at their height he was still writing his dazzling and iconoclastic comedies, the best-known of which is probably *The Recruiting Officer*.

Anne Oldfield began a long-term relationship with an MP named Arthur Mainwaring at around the same time as George's marriage. Her career went from strength to strength, and by the time she died in 1730 she was both rich and famous. She is buried in Westminster Abbey.

To Anne Oldfield, Sunday, after Sermon (1699?)

I came, I saw, and was conquered; never had man more to say, yet can I say nothing; where others go to save their souls, there have I lost mine; but I hope that Divinity which has the justest title to its service has received it; but I will endeavour to suspend these raptures for a moment, and talk calmly—

Nothing on earth, madam, can charm, beyond your wit but your beauty: after this not to love you would proclaim me a fool; and to say I did when I thought otherwise would pronounce me a knave; if anybody called me either I should resent it; and if you but think me either I shall break my heart.

You have already, madam, seen enough of me to create a liking or an aversion; your sense is above your sex, then let your proceeding be so likewise, and tell me plainly what I have to hope for. Were I to consult my merits my humility would chide any shadow of hope; but after a sight of such a face whose whole composition is a smile of good nature, why should I be so unjust as to suspect you of cruelty. Let me either live in *London* and be happy or retire again to my desert to check my vanity that drew me thence; but let me beg you to receive my sentence from your own mouth, that I may hear you speak and see you look at the same time; then let me be unfortunate if I can.

If you are not the lady in mourning that sat upon my right hand at church, you may go to the devil, for I'm sure you're a witch.

Alexander Pope
1688–1744

The brilliant Alexander Pope was a poet, critic, essayist, satirist, garden designer, art connoisseur, letter-writer and wit. He was dogged throughout his life by ill health; this was attributed to his spending too much time at his books, but in fact he had tuberculosis of the bone, contracted in infancy, which left him small, crippled and plagued with various tiresome ailments. He was a great feuder, but also had a large circle of devoted friends. He loved female society and was clearly extraordinarily charming, but while women enjoyed his attentions and his wit, his deeper feelings were never reciprocated.

Particular among his friends were two sisters, Martha and Teresa Blount, and he corresponded with both, writing at one point to Teresa, 'My violent passion for your fair self and your sister has been divided, and with the most wonderful regularity in the world. Even from my infancy I have been in love with one after the other of you week by week.' Pope never married, and Martha was the chief beneficiary of his will.

Four letters follow: one to each of the Blount

sisters, and two to Lady Mary Wortley Montagu, another intimate, married to a diplomat and living in Constantinople.

To Martha Blount, 1714

Most Divine,

It is some proof of my sincerity towards you, that I write when I am prepared by drinking to speak truth; and sure a letter after twelve at night must abound with that noble ingredient. That heart must have abundance of flames, which is at once warmed by wine and you: wine awakens and expresses the lurking passions of the mind, as varnish does the colours that are sunk in a picture, and brings them out in all their natural glowing. My good qualities have been so frozen and locked up in a dull constitution at all my former sober hours, that it is very astonishing to me, now I am drunk, to find so much virtue in me.

In these overflowings of my heart I pay you my thanks for these two obliging letters you favoured me with of the 18th and 24th instant. That which begins with 'My charming Mr Pope!' was a delight to me beyond all expression; you have at last entirely gained the conquest over your fair sister. It is true you are not handsome, for you are a woman, and think you are not: but this good humour and tenderness for me has a charm that cannot be resisted. That face must needs be irresistible which was adorned with smiles, even when it could not see the coronation! [of George I, in September 1714] I do suppose you will not show this epistle out of vanity, as I doubt not your sister does all I write to her . . .

To Teresa Blount, 1716

Madam,

– I have so much esteem for you, and so much of the other thing, that, were I a handsome fellow, I should do you a vast deal of good: but as it is, all I am good for, is to write a civil letter, or to make a fine speech. The truth is, that considering how often and how openly I have declared love to you, I am astonished (and a little affronted) that you have not forbid my correspondence, and directly said, *See my face no more!*

It is not enough, madam, for your reputation, that you have your hands pure from the stain of such ink as might be shed to gratify a male correspondent. Alas! While your heart consents to encourage him in this lewd liberty of writing, you are not (indeed you are not) what you would so fain have me think you – a prude! I am vain enough to conclude that (like most young fellows) a fine lady's silence is consent, and so I write on –

But, in order to be as innocent as possible in this epistle, I will tell you news. You have asked me news a thousand times, at the first word you spoke to me; which some would interpret as if you expected nothing from my lips: and truly it is not a sign two lovers are together, when they can be so impertinent as to inquire what the world does. All I mean by this is, that either you or I cannot be in love with the other: I leave you to guess which of the two is that stupid and insensible creature, so blind to the other's excellence and charms.

To Lady Mary Wortley Montagu, June 1717

Madam,
– If to live in the memory of others have anything desirable in it, 'tis what you possess with regard to me in the highest sense of the words.

There is not a day in which your figure does not appear before me; your conversations return to my thoughts, and every scene, place or occasion where I have enjoyed them, are as livelily painted as an imagination equally warm and tender can be capable to represent them.

You tell me, the pleasure of being nearer the sun has a great effect upon your health and spirits. You have turned my affections so far eastward that I could almost be one of his worshippers: for I think the sun has more reason to be proud of raising your spirits, than of raising all the plants, and ripening all the minerals in the earth.

It is my opinion, a reasonable man might gladly travel three or four thousand leagues to see your nature, and your wit, in their full perfection. What may not we expect from a creature that went over the most perfect of this part of the world, and is every day improving by the sun in the other. If you do not now write and speak the finest things imaginable, you must be content to be involved in the same imputation with the rest of the East and be concluded to have abandoned yourself to extreme effeminacy, laziness and lewdness of life . . .

For God's sake, madam, send to me as often as you can; in the dependence that there is no man breathing more constantly, or more anxiously mindful of you. Tell me that you are well, tell me that your little son is well, tell me that your very dog (if you have one) is well. Defraud me of no one thing that pleases you, for whatever that is, it will please me better than anything else can do. I am always yours.

To Lady Mary Wortley Montagu, after her return to England, 1719

I might be dead or you in Yorkshire, for anything that I am the better for your being in town. I have been sick ever since I saw you last, and now have a swelled face, and very bad; nothing will do me so much good as the sight of dear Lady Mary; when you come this way let me see you, for indeed I love you.

David Hume
1711–1776

David Hume was a philosopher, economist and historian; his great works include *A Treatise of Human Nature* and *An Enquiry Concerning Human Understanding*. He lived an exemplary scholarly life until 1763, when he visited Paris for the first time, and stayed for more than two years. He seems during this period to have suffered some kind of mid-life crisis; celebrated in the *salons* of the great Parisian ladies, he became particularly enamoured of one Madame de Boufflers, already the mistress of the prince de Conti. But the lady was a great deal more experienced than the philosopher in such flirtations, and the smitten Hume grew more and more confused. When her husband died, it became clear that she hoped to marry the prince, and Hume ultimately found himself in the rather unsatisfactory role of confidant to both.

To Madame de Boufflers, 3 April 1766

It is impossible for me, dear madam, to express the difficulty which I have to bear your absence, and the continual want which I feel of your society. I had accustomed myself, of a long time, to think of you as a friend from whom I was never to be separated during any considerable time; and I had flattered myself that we were fitted to pass our lives in intimacy and cordiality with each other. Age and a natural equality of temper were in danger of reducing my heart to too great indifference about everything, it was enlivened by the charms of your conversation, and the vivacity of your character. Your mind, more agitated both by unhappy circumstances in your situation and by your natural disposition, could repose itself in the more calm sympathy which you found with me.

But behold! three months are elapsed since I left you; and it is impossible for me to assign a time when I can hope to join you. I still return to my wish, that I had never left Paris, and that I had kept out of the reach of all other duties, except that which was so sweet, and agreeable, to fulfil, the cultivating your friendship and enjoying your society. Your obliging expressions revive this regret in the strongest degree; especially where you mention the wounds which, though skinned over, still fester at the bottom.

Oh! my dear friend, how I dread that it may still be long ere you reach a state of tranquillity, in a distress which so little admits of any remedy, and which the natural elevation of your character, instead of putting you above it, makes you feel with greater sensibility. I could only wish to administer the temporary consolation, which the presence of a friend never fails to afford . . . I kiss your hands with all the devotion possible.

Laurence Sterne
1713–1768

Laurence Sterne's masterpiece was *Tristram Shandy*, or, more properly, *The Life and Opinions of Tristram Shandy, Gentleman*, published in nine volumes between 1759 and 1767. It was an immediate success, and Sterne was fêted both at home and in Europe. The risqué wit and satire of *Tristram Shandy* shocked some readers, and seemed to them to be at odds with the author's profession; Sterne was a clergyman, and published several volumes of sermons. His paradoxical nature – the licentious moralist and sceptical Christian – is illustrated by the second letter here, to Lady Percy, in which he is trying hard to engineer a clandestine meeting while pretending to leave it all in the lap of the gods.

Sterne's marriage was widely known to be unhappy; his wife Elizabeth Lumley was described by her own cousin as 'a Woman of great integrity & many virtues, but they stand like quills upon the fretfull porcupine'. He had many love affairs, the most enduring with Catherine Fourmantel, a celebrated singer.

To Catherine Fourmantel, 8 May 1760

My dear Kitty,

– I have arrived here safe and sound except for the hole in my heart, which you have made, like a dear, enchanting slut as you are. And now my dear, dear girl! let me assure you of the truest friendship for you, that ever man bore towards a woman. Where ever I am, my heart is warm towards you and ever shall be till it is cold for ever.

I thank you for the kind proof you gave me of your love and of your desire to make my heart easy, in ordering yourself to be denied to you know who: – whilst I ham [sic] so miserable to be separated from my dear dear Kitty, it would have stabbed my soul to have thought such a fellow could have the liberty of comeing near you. I therefore take this proof of your love and good principles most kindly, and have as much faith and dependence upon you in it as if I were at your elbow – would to God I was at it this moment! but I am sitting solitary and alone in my bedchamber (ten o'clock at night after the play) and would give a guinea for a squeeze of your hand. I send my soul perpetually out to see what you are a-doing – wish I could send my body with it.

Adieu! dear and kind girl, and believe me ever your kind friend and most affectionate admirer. I go to the Oratorio this night. Adieu! Adieu!

P.S. –My service to your Mama.

Direct to me in the Pall Mal at ye 2nd House from St Alban's Street

There is a strange mechanical effect produced in writing a billet-doux within a stone cast of the lady who engrosses the heart and soul of an *inamoratos*. For this cause (but mostly because I am to dine in this neighbourhood) have I, Tristram Shandy, come forth from my lodgings to a coffee-house, the nearest I could find to my dear Lady's house, and have called for a sheet of gilt paper to try the truth of this article of my creed – now for it –

O my dear Lady, what a dishclout of a soul has thou made of me! – I think, by the by, this a little too familiar an introduction for so unfamiliar a situation as I stand in with you – where, heaven knows, I am kept at a distance and despair of getting an inch nearer you, with all the steps and windings I can think of to recommend myself to you. Would not any man in his senses run diametrically from you, and as far as his legs would carry him, rather than thus causelessly, foolishly and foolhardily, expose himself afresh and afresh, where his heart and his reason tell him he shall be sure to come off loser, if not totally undone.

Why would you tell me you would be glad to see me? Does it give you pleasure to make me more unhappy, or does it add to your triumph, that your eyes and lips have turned a man into a fool, whom the rest of the town is courting as a wit?

I am a fool, the weakest, the most ductile, the most

tender fool that ever woman tried the weakness of, and the most unsettled in my purposes and resolutions of recovering my right mind.

It is but an hour ago that I kneeled down and swore I never would come near you, and after saying my Lord's Prayer for the sake of the close, *of not being led into temptation*, out I sallied like any Christian hero, ready to take the field against the world, the flesh and the devil; not doubting but I should finally trample them all down under my feet.

And now I am got so near you, within this vile stone's cast of your house, I feel myself drawn into a vortex, that has turned my brain upside downwards; and though I had purchased a box ticket to carry me to Miss —'s benefit, yet I knew very well that was a single line directed to me to let me know Lady — would be alone at seven, and suffer me to spend the evening with her, she would infallibly see everything verified as I have told her.

I dine at Mr C—r's in Wigmore Street, in this neighbourhood, where I shall stay till seven, in hopes you purpose to put me to this proof. If I hear nothing by that time, I shall conclude you are better disposed of, and shall take a sorry hack and sorrily jog on to the play. Curse on the word, I know nothing but sorrow, except the one thing that I love you (perhaps foolishly, but) most sincerely,

L. Sterne

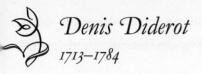

Denis Diderot
1713–1784

Denis Diderot, philosopher, novelist and polymath, was born in the eastern French city of Langres. After gaining his degree, he abandoned his original plan to study for the priesthood, and instead started studying law; he abandoned this in turn in 1734, and declared his intention to become a writer, thus alienating his family. They were further alienated by his marriage to Antoinette Champion, a devout Roman Catholic, whom they regarded as socially inferior, poorly educated and too old (she was four years his senior). In the event, the marriage was not happy, and in 1755 Diderot began a love affair with Sophie Volland, which lasted until her death.

As is the case with many Great Men, Diderot was always short of money. He spent almost twenty-five years compiling one of the first encyclopaedias, a project which the French authorities saw as dangerously seditious, and Diderot was constantly harassed as he worked on it. In the end, Catherine the Great of Russia, hearing of his money troubles, offered to buy his library; she then told him it was to be kept in Paris, and she would pay him as its custodian. After his death, the library was shipped to St Petersburg, where today it remains in the collection of the National Library of Russia.

To Sophie Volland, July 1759

I cannot leave this place without saying a few words to you. So, my pet, you expect a good deal from me. Your happiness, your life, even, depend, you say, upon my ever loving you!

Never fear, my dear Sophie; that will endure, and you shall live, and be happy. I have never committed a crime yet, and am not going to begin. I am wholly yours – you are everything to me; we will sustain each other in all the ills of life it may please fate to inflict upon us; you will soothe my troubles; I will comfort you in yours. Would that I could always see you as you have been lately! As for myself, you must confess that I am just as I was on the first day you saw me.

This is no merit of my own; but I owe it in justice to myself to tell you so. It is one effect of good qualities to be felt more vividly from day to day. Be assured of my constancy to yours, and of my appreciation of them. Never was a passion more justified by reason than mine. Is it not true, my dear Sophie, that you are very amiable? Examine yourself – see how worthy you are of being loved; and know that I love you very much. That is the unvarying standard of my feelings.

Good night, my dear Sophie. I am as happy as man can be in knowing that I am loved by the best of women.

To Sophie Volland, Au Grandval, 20 October 1759

You are well! You think of me! You love me. You will always love me. I believe you: now I am happy. I live again. I can talk, work, play, walk – do anything you wish. I must have made myself very disagreeable the last two or three days. No! my love; your very presence would not have delighted me more than your first letter did.

How impatiently I waited for it! I am sure my hands trembled when opening it. My countenance changed; my voice altered; and unless he were a fool, he who handed it to me would have said – 'That man receives news from his father or mother, or someone else he loves.' I was just at that moment about to send you a letter expressing my great uneasiness. While you are amusing yourself, you forget how much my heart suffers . . .

Adieu, my dearest love. My affection for you is ardent and sincere. I would love you even more than I do, if I knew how.

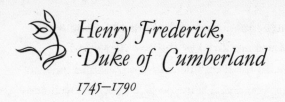

Henry Frederick, Duke of Cumberland
1745–1790

Henry Frederick was the brother of George III. His affair with the married Henrietta Vernon, Lady Grosvenor, caused a great scandal; the lovers were not discreet, and the Duke pursued Lady Grosvenor up and down the country disguised as first 'a Welshman' (whatever that entailed) and then 'a farmer'. Lord Grosvenor brought an action for 'criminal conversation' (adultery) against him, and the jury, having been shown some of the lovers' correspondence, awarded damages against the Duke of £10,000. The letters were stolen, published and caused a sensation all over London. As this one demonstrates, the Duke's ardour was great, if somewhat inarticulate.

To Lady Grosvenor

My dear little Angel,
– I wrote my last letter to you yesterday at eleven o'clock just when we sailed I dined at two o'clock and as for the afternoon I had some music I have my own servant a-board that plays

... and so got to bed about 10 – I then prayed for you *my dearest love kissed your dearest little hair* and laye down and dreamt of you had you on the dear little *couch* ten thousand times in my arms kissing you and telling you how much I loved and adored you and you seem pleased but alas when I woke it found it all dillusion *nobody by me but myself at sea* ... I am sure the account of this days duty can be no pleasure to you my love yet it is exactly what I have done and as I promised you always to let you know my motions and thoughts I have now performed my promise this day to you and always will until the very last letter you shall have from me.

When I shall return to you that instant O' my love mad and happy beyond myself to tell you how I love you and have thought of you ever since I have been separated from you ... I hope you are well I am sure I need not tell you I have had nothing in my thoughts but your dearself and long for the time to come back again to you I will all the while take care of myself because you desire *my dear little Friend* does the angel of my heart pray do you take care of your dearself for the sake of your faithful servant who lives but to love you to adore you, and to bless the moment that has made you generous enough to own it to him I hope my dear nay I will dare to say you never will have reason to repent it ...

Indeed my dear angel I need not tell you I know you read the reason too well that made me do so it was to write to you for God knows I wrote to no one else nor shall I at any other but to the King God bless you most amiable and dearest little creature living ...

God bless you till I shall again have an opportunity of sending to you, I shall write to you a letter a day as many days as you miss herein of me when I do they shall all come Friday 16th June God bless I shant forget you God knows you have told me so before I have your heart and it lies warm at my breast I hope mine feels as easy to you thou joy of my life adieu.

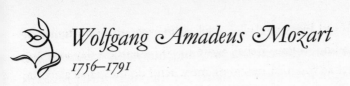

Wolfgang Amadeus Mozart
1756–1791

Wolfgang Amadeus Mozart was one of the most talented, prolific and influential composers the world has ever seen. He was born in Salzburg, and was playing and composing from the age of five. He spent a great deal of his childhood touring the courts of Europe with his family, astounding audiences with his precocity.

The opportunities in Salzburg for a musician and composer of his breadth and brilliance were limited, and it was on a later trip around Europe, at Mannheim in Germany, that Mozart met and fell in love with Aloysia Weber, a singer. They were parted when he returned home, and when they met again two years later, Aloysia was no longer interested in him, and according to some accounts failed even to recognize him.

A few years later, in Vienna, Mozart encountered the Weber family again. Aloysia had married an actor, and Mozart turned his attention to her younger sister, Constanze, whom he married in 1782; they had six children, only two of whom survived infancy.

The Mozarts' fortunes fell and rose according to fashion and whether or not Mozart felt like writing the music that would please his potential patrons. They were undoubtedly extravagant, and inevitably posterity has sought to blame Constanze for their perennial problems with money. The letters between them suggest though that their marriage was a happy one, and they seem to have shared a childlike sense of humour (Mozart's jokes were almost obsessively scatological). Constanze accompanied Mozart on many of his numerous trips abroad, and after his tragic early death worked hard to preserve his legacy and enhance his reputation.

To Constanze, sent from Dresden, 16 April 1789

Dear little wife, I have a number of requests to make. I beg you

(1) not to be melancholy,
(2) to take care of your health and to beware of the spring breezes,
(3) not to go out walking alone – and preferably not to go out walking at all,
(4) to feel absolutely assured of my love. Up to the present I have not written a single letter to you without placing your dear portrait before me.
(6)* and lastly I beg you to send me more details in your

*Paragraphs 5 and 6 reversed in copy of letter in Berlin Library letters. I should very much like to know whether our brother-in-law Hofer came to see us the day after my departure? Whether he comes very often, as he promised me he would? Whether the Langes come sometimes? Whether progress is being made with the portrait? What sort of life you are leading? All these things are naturally of great interest to me.

(5) I beg in your conduct not only to be careful of your honour and mine, but also to consider appearances. Do not be angry with me for asking this. You ought to love me even more for thus valuing our honour.

W. A. Mozart

To Constanze, sent from Vienna, 6 June 1791

I have this moment received your dear letter and am delighted to hear that you are well and in good spirits. Madame Leutgeb has laundered my nightcap and neck-tie, but I should like you to see them! Good God! I kept on telling her, '*Do let me show you how she (my wife) does them!*' – But it was no use. I am delighted that you have a good appetite – but whoever gorges a lot, must also shit a lot – no, walk a lot, I mean. But I should not like you to take *long walks* without me. I entreat you to follow my advice exactly, for it comes from my heart. Adieu – my love – my only one. Do catch them in the air – those 2999½ little kisses from me which are flying about, waiting for someone to snap them up. Listen, I want to whisper something in your ear – and you in mine – and now we open and close our mouths – again – again and again – at last we say: 'It is all about Plumpi – Strumpi – ' Well, you can think what you like – that is just why it's so convenient. Adieu. A thousand tender kisses. Ever your

Mozart

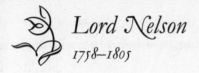

Lord Nelson
1758–1805

The legendary love affair between Lord Nelson and the great beauty Emma Hamilton began in Naples in 1798, where Emma was living with her husband, Sir William Hamilton, a diplomat more than thirty years her senior. Until her marriage, Emma had scraped by with jobs as an actress and artists' model and a murky career in London's *demi-monde*; she had been passed like a parcel to Sir William by his nephew, who had grown tired of her and who needed to marry an heiress, not a penniless courtesan. Sir William then confounded everyone by actually marrying Emma, for whom he seems to have had a genuine and deep regard.

Sir William also seems to have tolerated his wife's relationship with the naval hero quite happily, and the three of them lived as a *ménage-à-trois* after the Hamiltons' return to London in 1800. At the end of 1801, Emma gave birth to Nelson's daughter, Horatia.

Sir William died in 1803; Nelson in 1805 at the Battle of Trafalgar. His last letter to Emma, the second below, was found on his desk on HMS *Victory*; on it, Lady Hamilton has written, 'O miserable wretched Emma! O glorious and happy Nelson!'.

Despite Nelson's provisions for her in his will, and his pleas to his government to look after her should he be killed in battle, Emma was arrested and sent to debtor's prison in 1813. She escaped in 1814 and fled with Horatia to Calais, where she died in poverty the following year, probably of cirrhosis of the liver.

To Lady Hamilton

My Dearest Emma,

All your letters, *my dear letters*, are so entertaining, and which point so clearly what you are after that they give me either the greatest pleasure or pain. It is the next best thing to being with you.

I only desire, my dearest Emma, that you will always believe that Nelson's your own; Nelson's Alpha and Omega is Emma! I cannot alter – my affection and love is beyond even this world! Nothing will shake it but yourself; and that I will not allow myself to think for a moment is possible.

I feel that you are the real friend of my bosom, and dearer to me than life; and that I am the same to you. But I will neither have P's nor Q's come near you. No, not the slice of a single Gloster. But if I was to go on, it would argue that want of confidence which would be injurious to your honour.

I rejoice that you have had so pleasant a trip into Norfolk, and I hope one day to carry you there by a nearer *tie* in law, but not in love and affection than at present . . .

To Lady Hamilton
Victory, *19 October 1805, noon; Cadiz, SSE 16 leagues*

My dearest beloved Emma and the dear friends of my bosom, –The signal has been made that the enemy's combined fleet is coming out of port.

We have very little wind, so that I have no hopes of seeing them before to-morrow. May the God of Battles crown my endeavours with success! At all events I shall take care that my name shall ever be most dear to you and Horatia, both of whom I love as much as my own life; and as my last writing before the battle will be to you, so I hope in God that I shall live to finish my letter after the battle. May Heaven keep you, prays your Nelson and Bronte.

October 20th –In the morning we were close to the mouth of the straights, but the wind had not come far enough to the westward to allow the combined fleets to weather the shoals of Trafalgar, but they were counted as far as forty sail of ships-of-war which I suppose to be thirty-four of the line and six frigates. A group of them was seen off the lighthouse of Cadiz this morning, but it blows so very fresh, I think . . . that I rather believe they will go into harbour before night.

May God Almighty give us success over these fellows and enable us to get a Peace.

Robert Burns
1759–1796

Robert Burns was a poet of great repute when he met Mrs Agnes Maclehose at an Edinburgh tea party in 1787. Agnes ('Nancy') was married to James Maclehose, a Glasgow law agent, but had left him because of his cruelty and returned to Edinburgh. Almost at once she and Burns began a passionate correspondence and possibly a full-blown love affair. They used the pen-names 'Sylvander' and 'Clarinda' to protect their identities should their letters be discovered.

Burns was a hopeless (or, alternatively, terrific) womanizer, and rather impressively managed to impregnate Mrs Maclehose's maidservant Jenny Clow at the same time as carrying on the heated correspondence with her mistress. He was also maintaining a relationship with Jean Armour in Ayrshire, who had borne him twins in 1786 and was once again pregnant. In 1791, Mrs Maclehose and Robert Burns parted for the last time, and in 1792, she sailed for Jamaica, where her husband now lived, in order to try for a reconciliation. The attempt failed, and she returned to Edinburgh three months later, where she remained until her death in 1841.

To Mrs Agnes Maclehose, Tuesday evening, 15 January 1788

That you have faults, my Clarinda, I never doubted; but I knew not where they existed; and Saturday night made me more in the dark than ever. O, Clarinda! why would you wound my soul, by hinting that last night must have lessened my opinion of you. True, I was behind the scenes with you; but what did I see? A bosom glowing with honour and benevolence; a mind ennobled by genius, informed and refined by education and reflection, and exalted by native religion, genuine as in the climes of Heaven; a heart formed for all the glorious meltings of friendship, love, and pity. These I saw. I saw the noblest immortal soul creation ever showed me.

I looked long, my dear Clarinda, for your letter; and am vexed that you are complaining. I have not caught you so far wrong as in your idea – that the commerce you have with one friend hurts you, if you cannot tell every tittle of it to another. Why have so injurious a suspicion of a good God, Clarinda, as to think that Friendship and Love, on the sacred, inviolate principles of Truth, Honour and Religion, can be anything else than an object of His divine approbation? I have mentioned, in some of my former scrawls, Saturday evening next. Do allow me to wait on you that evening. Oh, my angel! how soon must we part! And when can we meet again! I look forward on the horrid interval with tearful eyes. What have not I lost by not knowing you sooner!

I fear, I fear, my acquaintance with you is too short to make that lasting impression on your heart I could wish.

Sylvander

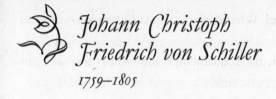

Johann Christoph Friedrich von Schiller

1759–1805

Schiller was a German poet, dramatist, historian and translator. He met Charlotte von Lengefeld in 1785, with her sister Karoline; after a correspondence of several years, Schiller married Charlotte in February 1790. This letter dates from August 1789, seven months before their wedding; evidently Schiller had asked Karoline to intercede for him with Charlotte, and had received an encouraging reply. Schiller and Charlotte had four children; he was troubled by ill-health for much of his life, and Charlotte outlived him by twenty years.

To Charlotte von Lengefeld, 3 August 1789

Is it true, dearest Lotte? May I hope that Karoline has read in your soul and has answered me out of your heart, what I did not have the courage to confess? Oh, how hard this secret has become for me, that I, as long as we have known each other, have had to conceal! Often, when we still lived together, I collected my whole courage and came to you with the intention to disclose it to you – but this courage always forsook me. I thought to discover selfishness in my wish, I feared that I had only my happiness in view, and that thought drove me back. Could I not become *to you* what you were to me, then my suffering would have distressed you, and I would have destroyed the most beautiful harmony of our friendship through my confession. I would have also lost that, what I had, your true and sisterly friendship. And yet again there come moments, when my hope arose afresh, wherein the happiness, which we could give each other, seemed to me exalted above every, every consideration, when I considered it even as noble to sacrifice everything else to it. You could be happy without me – but not become unhappy through me. This I felt alive in me – and thereupon I built my hopes.

You could give yourself to another, but none could love you more purely or more completely than I did. To none could your happiness be holier, as it was to me, and always will be. My whole existence, everything that lives within me, everything, my most precious, I devote to you, and if I try to ennoble myself, that is done, in order to become ever worthier of you, to make you ever happier. Nobility of souls is a beautiful and indestructible bond of friendship and of love. Our friendship and love become indestructible and eternal like the feelings upon which we establish them.

Now forget everything that could put constraint on your heart, and allow your feelings to speak alone. Confirm to me, what Karoline had allowed me hope. Tell me that you will be *mine* and that my happiness costs you no sacrifice.

Oh, assure me of that, it only needs a single word. Our hearts have a long time been close to each other. Allow the only foreign element which has hitherto been between us to vanish, and nothing, nothing to disturb the free communion of our souls. Farewell, dearest Lotte! I yearn for a quiet moment, to portray to you all the feeling of my heart, which, during that long period that this longing alone dwells in my heart, have made me happy and then again unhappy ... Do not delay to banish my unrest for ever and always, I give all the pleasures of my life into your hand ... Farewell, my most precious!

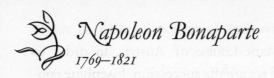

Napoleon Bonaparte
1769–1821

Napoleon, the humble soldier from Corsica who became a great general and Emperor of France, married Joséphine de Beauharnais in March 1796. She was an impoverished Creole aristocrat from the French colony of Martinique with two children from an earlier marriage.

The first three letters here were written shortly after their wedding, when Napoleon had become commander of the French forces in Italy; the fourth dates from the Austrian war of 1805. In these letters, Napoleon casts himself as the supplicant, at the mercy of his beautiful and hard-hearted wife, who sometimes even insists on using the formal *vous* instead of the affectionate *tu*; there is something touching and almost comical about his anxious pursuit of Joséphine all over Italy while conducting the military campaign that would make his name. It became clear to both later on in their marriage that neither had remained faithful, and Joséphine's extravagance was a constant source of friction between them, but it seems from these early letters that Napoleon was very much in love with his wife.

Napoleon divorced Joséphine in 1810 to marry Archduchess Marie-Louise of Austria, in order to gain an heir and secure the succession. Joséphine continued to live near Paris, and remained on good terms with her former husband until she died in 1814.

After his defeat by the British, Napoleon was exiled to the island of St Helena in 1815, where he died six years later.

To Joséphine at Milan,
Sent from Verona, 13 November 1796

I do not love thee any more; on the contrary, I detest thee. Thou art horrid, very awkward, very stupid, a very Cinderella. Thou dost not write me at all, thou dost not love thy husband; thou knowest the pleasure that thy letters afford him, and thou dost not write him six lines of even haphazard scribble.

What do you do then all day, Madame? What matter of such importance is it that takes up your time from writing to your very good lover? What affection stifles and pushes on one side the love, the tender and constant love, which you have promised him? Who can be this marvellous, this new lover who absorbs all your instants, tyrannises your entire days, and prevents you from being solicitous about your husband? Joséphine, beware, one fine night the doors will break open and I will be there.

In truth, I am anxious, my good *amie*, at not receiving your news; write me quickly four pages, and say those amiable things which fill my heart with sentiment and pleasure.

I hope before long to press you in my arms and shall shower on you a million burning kisses as under the Equator.

Bonaparte

To Joséphine at Genoa
Sent from Milan, 27 November 1796, three o'clock afternoon

I arrive at Milan, I rush into your *appartement*, I have left everything to see you, to press you in my arms . . . you were not there; you run to towns where there are festivities; you leave me when I arrive, you do not care any more for your dear Napoleon. It was a caprice, your loving him; fickleness makes you indifferent to him. Accustomed to dangers, I know the remedy for the worries and ills of life. The misfortune that overtakes me is incalculable; I had the right to be spared this.

I shall be here till the 9th in the evening. Do not put yourself out; run after pleasures; happiness is made for you. The entire world is too glad to be able to please you, and only your husband is very, very unhappy.

Bonaparte

I have not spent a day without loving you; I have not spent a night without embracing you; I have not so much as drunk one cup of tea without cursing the pride and ambition which force me to remain apart from the moving spirit of my life. In the midst of my duties, whether I am at the head of my army or inspecting the camps, my beloved Joséphine stands alone in my heart, occupies my mind, fills my thoughts. If I am moving away from you with the speed of the Rhône torrent, it is only that I may see you again more quickly. If I rise to work in the middle of the night, it is because this may hasten by a matter of days the arrival of my sweet love. Yet in your letter of the 23rd and 26th Ventôse, you call me *vous*. *Vous* yourself! Ah! wretch, how could you have written this letter? How cold it is! And then there are those four days between the 23rd and the 26th; what were you doing that you failed to write to your husband? . . . Ah, my love, that *vous*, those four days make me long for my former indifference. Woe to the person responsible! May he, as punishment and penalty, experience what my convictions and the evidence (which is in your friend's favour) would make me experience! Hell has no torments great enough! Nor do the Furies have serpents enough! *Vous!* *Vous!* Ah! how will things stand in two weeks? . . . My spirit is heavy; my heart is fettered and I am terrified by my fantasies . . . You love me less; but you will get over the loss. One day you will love me no longer; at least tell me; then I shall know how I have come to deserve this misfortune . . . Farewell, my wife: the torment, joy, hope and moving spirit of my life; whom I love, whom I fear, who fills me with tender feelings which draw me close to Nature, and with violent impulses as tumultuous as thunder. I ask of you neither eternal love, nor fidelity, but simply . . . *truth*, unlimited honesty. The day when you say 'I love you less', will mark the end of my love and the last day of my life. If my heart were base enough to love without being loved in return I would tear it to pieces. Joséphine! Joséphine! Remember what I have sometimes said to you: Nature has endowed me with a virile and decisive character. It has built yours out of lace and gossamer. Have you ceased to love me? Forgive me, love of my life, my soul is racked by conflicting forces.

My heart, obsessed by you, is full of fears which prostrate me with misery . . . I am distressed not to be calling you by name. I shall wait for you to write it.

Farewell! Ah! if you love me less you can never have loved me. In that case I shall truly be pitiable.

Bonaparte

P.S. –The war this year has changed beyond recognition. I have had meat, bread and fodder distributed; my armed cavalry will soon be on the march. My soldiers are showing inexpressible confidence in me; you alone are a source of chagrin to me; you alone are the joy and torment of my life. I send a kiss to your children, whom you do not mention. By God! If you did, your letters would be half as long again.

Then visitors at ten o'clock in the morning would not have the pleasure of seeing you. Woman!!!

To Joséphine at Munich, 19 December 1805

Great Empress, not a letter from you since your departure from Strassburg. You have passed at Baden, at Stuttgart, at Munich, without writing us a word. That is not very admirable nor very tender! I am still at Brunn. The Russians are gone; I have a truce. In a few days I shall decide what I shall do. Deign from the height of your greatness, to occupy yourself a little of your slaves.

    Napoleon

Daniel Webster
1782–1852

This letter, from Daniel Webster, American orator and statesman (and martyr to hay fever), might not strictly conform to what we think of as a love letter, but it is one of enormous affection and charm, written with such wit and grace to a young woman who had left her bonnet at his house after attending dinner there, that it seems worthy of inclusion.

To Josephine Seaton, 4 March 1844

My Dear Josephine,

I fear you got a wetting last evening, as it rained fast soon after you left our door; and I avail myself of the return of your bonnet, to express the wish that you are well this morning, and without cold.

I have demanded parlance with your Bonnet: have asked it how many tender looks it has noticed to be directed under it; what soft words it has heard, close to its side; in what instances an air of triumph has caused it to be tossed; and whether, ever, and when, it has quivered from trembling emotions, proceeding from below. But it has proved itself a faithful keeper of secrets, and would answer none of my questions. It only remained for me to attempt to surprise it into confession, by pronouncing sundry names, one after another. It seemed quite unmoved by most of these, but at the apparently unexpected mention of one, I thought its ribands decidedly fluttered!

I gave it my parting good wishes; hoping that it might never cover an aching head, and that the eyes which it protects from the rays of the sun, may know no tears but those of joy and affection.

Yours, dear Josephine, with affectionate regard.

Danl. Webster

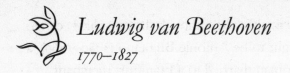

Ludwig van Beethoven
1770–1827

Ludwig van Beethoven revolutionized music and moved it on from the realm of aristocratic patronage – he was one of the first composers to rely on earnings rather than assorted rich benefactors for his living. His combative nature is shown by the dedication of his Third Symphony; originally it was to Napoleon, an almost exact contemporary and sometime hero, but then Napoleon declared himself Emperor, which so enraged Beethoven that he dedicated it instead to 'the *memory* of a great man'.

Beethoven's life was blighted by his increasing deafness – an unimaginably terrible affliction for a composer of his genius, and one which led him to the brink of suicide. He was by all accounts difficult, tortured, depressed and irascible – hardly surprising in the circumstances. He never married, although did fall deeply in love more than once, usually with one of his aristocratic and unattainable pupils.

Three passionate unsent love letters were found among Beethoven's papers after his death, addressed to his 'Immortal Beloved'. There was no year on the letters, and the identity of the 'Immortal Beloved' has not been conclusively established, although the most likely candidate is thought to be Antonie Brentano (1780–1869), a Viennese woman married to a Frankfurt merchant.

To 'Immortal Beloved', 6 July, morning

My angel, my all, my own self – only a few words to-day, and that too with pencil (with yours) – only till to-morrow is my lodging definitely fixed. What abominable waste of time in such things – why this deep grief, where necessity speaks? Can our love persist otherwise than through sacrifices, than by not demanding everything? Canst thou change it, that thou are not entirely mine, I not entirely thine? Oh, God, look into beautiful Nature and compose your mind to the inevitable. Love demands everything and is quite right, so it is *for me with you*, for *you with me* – only you forget so easily, that I must live *for you and for me* – were we quite united, you would notice this painful feeling as little as I should . . .

. . . We shall probably soon meet, even to-day I cannot communicate my remarks to you, which during these days I made about my life – were our hearts close together, I should probably not make any such remarks. My bosom is full, to tell you much – there are moments when I find that speech is nothing at all. Brighten up – remain my true and only treasure, my all, as I to you. The rest the gods must send, what must be for us and shall.

    Your faithful

    Ludwig

Monday evening, 6 July

You suffer, you, my dearest creature. Just now I perceive that letters must be posted first thing early. Mondays – Thursdays – the only days, when the post goes from here to K. You suffer – oh! Where I am, you are with me, with me and you, I shall arrange that I may live with you. What a life! So! Without you – pursued by the kindness of the people here and there, whom I mean – to desire to earn just as little as they earn – humility of man towards men – it pains me – and when I regard myself in connection with the Universe, what I am, and what he is – whom one calls the greatest – and yet – there lies herein again the godlike of man. I weep when I think you will probably only receive on Saturday the first news from me – as you too love – yet I love you stronger – but never hide yourself from me. Good night – as I am taking the waters, I must go to bed. Oh God – so near! so far! Is it not a real building of heaven, our Love – but as firm, too, as the citadel of heaven.

Good morning, on 7 July

Even in bed my ideas yearn towards you, my Immortal Beloved, here and there joyfully, then again sadly, awaiting from Fate, whether it will listen to us. I can only live, either altogether with you or not at all. Yes, I have determined to wander about for so long far away, until I can fly into your arms and call myself quite at home with you, can send my soul enveloped by yours into the realm of spirits – yes, I regret, it must be. You will get over it all the more as you know my faithfulness to you; never another one can own my heart, never – never! O God, why must one go away from what one loves so, and yet my life in W. as it is now is a miserable life. Your love made me the happiest and unhappiest at the same time. At my actual age I should need some continuity, sameness of life – can that exist under our circumstances? Angel, I just hear that the post goes out every day – and must close therefore, so that you get the L. at once. Be calm – love me – to-day – yesterday.

What longing in tears for you – You – my Life – my All – farewell. Oh, go on loving me – never doubt the faithfullest heart

Of your beloved

L

Ever thine.

Ever mine.

Ever ours.

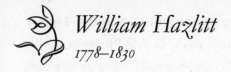

William Hazlitt
1778–1830

William Hazlitt was an essayist and critic who wrote on a variety of subjects from literature to prizefighting. His work was mocked by the same reactionary critics who tormented the poet John Keats; calling him 'Bill Hazlitt', they sneered at him as a failed artist and a 'manufacturer' of essays. His reputation undoubtedly suffered as a result of this, but also as a result of an unfortunate infatuation.

Hazlitt had married Sarah Stoddart, the daughter of a naval lieutenant, in 1808; by 1820, they had separated, and Hazlitt moved into rented rooms off Chancery Lane. It was here, on the morning of 16 August, that the twenty-year-old Sarah Walker, the landlady's daughter, brought him his breakfast. He fell instantly in love with her, and for the next three years rather lost his head. He decided he must have a divorce; remarriage after divorce was possible only under Scottish law, and so he set off for Scotland. While waiting in Edinburgh for the case to be completed, he rushed back intermittently to London, only to be consumed with jealousy at the idea that Sarah Walker was carrying on with another lodger called

John Tomkins. Sarah, to the puzzlement of Hazlitt (and presumably no one else), avoided him; he spent his time either trying to win her back or catch her out, at one point hiring an acquaintance to take a room in Chancery Lane to try to seduce her.

Hazlitt wrote a book about the whole experience, *Liber Amoris*, and although it was published anonymously, word of its authorship quickly got out. It was a gift to Hazlitt's enemies in the press – excruciatingly embarrassing and entirely lacking in dignity. And as a final humiliation, in 1824, Sarah had a son by Tomkins, with whom she lived until his death in 1858; she herself died twenty years later.

To Sarah Walker

– You will scold me for this, and ask me if this is keeping my promise to mind my work. One half of it was to think of Sarah; and besides I do not neglect my work either I assure you. I regularly do ten pages a day, which mounts up to thirty guineas' worth a week, so that you see I should grow rich at this rate, if I could keep on so; *and I could keep on so*, if I had you with me to encourage me with your sweet smiles, and share my lot. The Berwick smacks sail twice a week, and the wind sets fair. When I think of the thousand endearing caresses that have passed between us, I do not wonder at the strong attachment that draws me to you, but I am sorry for my own want of power to please. I hear the wind sigh through the lattice and keep repeating over and over to myself two lines of Lord Byron's tragedy –

So shalt thou find me ever at thy side,

Here and hereafter, if the last may be,

applying them to thee, my love, and thinking whether I shall ever see thee again. Perhaps not – for some years at least – till both thou and I are old – and then when all else have forsaken thee, I will creep to thee, and die in thine arms.

You once made me believe I was not hated by her I loved: and for that sensation – so delicious was it, though but a mockery and a dream – I owe you more than I can ever pay. I thought to have dried up my tears for ever the day I left you: but as I write this they stream again. If they did not, I think my heart would burst.

I walk out here on an afternoon and hear the notes of the thrush that comes up from a sheltered valley below, welcome in the spring; but they do not melt my heart as they used; it is grown cold and dead. As you say it will one day be colder. God forgive what I have written above; I did not intend it; but you were once my little all, and I cannot bear the thought of having lost your forever, I fear through my own fault. Has any one called? Do not send any letters that come. I should like you and your mother (if agreeable) to go and see Mr Kean in 'Othello' and Miss Stephens in 'Love in a Village', if you will, I will write to Mr T— to send you tickets. Has Mr P— called? I think I must send to him for the picture to kiss and talk to. Kiss me my best beloved. Ah! if you can never be mine, still let me be your proud and happy slave.

H.

Lord Byron
1788–1824

'Byronic' has become shorthand for a particular type of romantic hero – pale, dark-haired, hollow-cheeked, cruel, reckless, irresistible to many women and therefore a source of deep irritation to the better behaved and more reliable sort of man so often and so inexplicably overlooked. Byron's behaviour, and his poetry, scandalized large parts of Europe to the extent that in 1924, a hundred years after his death, a petition for a memorial to him in Westminster Abbey was refused by the dean, whose opinion it was that 'Byron, partly by his openly dissolute life and partly by the influence of his licentious verse, earned a world-wide reputation for immorality among English-speaking people'.

Of the many entanglements of Byron's life, one of the most notorious was with the married Lady Caroline Lamb; in July 1813, it was rumoured that following a quarrel with him at a party, she tried to stab herself first with a knife, then with a broken glass. Eventually, she withdrew to Ireland, and the letter that follows was written to her there. The second letter was written to the Countess Guiccioli, a young woman married to a much older man, whom Byron met in

Venice in 1819; Byron inscribed his declaration on the flyleaf of a novel she had lent him.

To Lady Caroline Lamb

My dearest Caroline,
– If the tears, which you saw, and I know I am not apt to shed; if the agitation in which I parted from you – agitation which you must have perceived through the whole of this nervous affair, did not commence till the moment of leaving you approached; if all I have said and done, and am still but too ready to say and do, have not sufficiently proved what my feelings are, and must ever be, towards you, my love, I have no other proof to offer.

God knows I never knew till this moment the madness of my dear dearest and most beloved friend. I cannot express myself, this is no time for words – but I shall have a pride, a melancholy pleasure, in suffering what you yourself can scarcely conceive, for you do not know me.

I am about to go out with a heavy heart, for my appearing this evening will stop any absurd story to which the events of the day might give rise. Do you think now I am cold and stern and wilful? Will ever others think so? Will your mother ever? The mother to whom we must indeed sacrifice much more, much more on my part than she shall ever know, or can imagine.

'Promise not to love you'? Ah, Caroline, it is past promising! But I shall attribute all concessions to the proper motive, and never cease to feel all that you have already witnessed, and more than ever can be known, but to my own heart – perhaps, to yours. May God forgive, protect and bless you ever and ever, more than ever. –Your most attached

Byron

P.S. –These taunts have driven you to this, my dearest Caroline, and were it not for your mother, and the kindness of your connexions, is there anything in heaven or earth that would have made me so happy as to have made you mine long ago? And not less now than then, but more than ever *at this time*.

God knows I wish you happy, and when I quit you, or rather you, from a sense of duty to your husband and mother, quit me, you shall acknowledge the truth of what I again promise and vow, that no other, in word nor deed, shall ever hold the place in my affections which is and shall be sacred to you till I am nothing. You know I would with pleasure give up all here or beyond the grave for you, and in refraining from this must my motives be misunderstood?

I care not who knows this, what use is made of it – it is to you and to you only, yourself. I was, and am yours, freely and entirely, to obey, to honour, love and fly with you, *when*, *where*, and *how*, yourself might and may determine.

To the Countess Guiccioli, 25 August 1819

My dearest Teresa,

– I have read this book in your garden. My love, you were absent, or else I could not have read it. It is a favourite book of yours, and the writer was a favourite friend of mine. You will not understand these English words, and others will not understand them . . . which is the reason I have not scrawled them in Italian. But you will recognise the handwriting of him who passionately loved you, and you will divine that, over a book which was yours, he could only think of love.

In that word, beautiful in all languages, but most in yours – *amor mio* – is comprised my existence here and hereafter. I feel I exist here; and I feel I shall exist hereafter, to *what* purpose you will decide; my destiny rests with you, and you are a woman, seventeen years of age, and two out of a convent, I wish you had stayed there, with all my heart, or at least, that I had never met you in your married state. But all this is too late, I love you, and you love me – at least you *say* so, and *act*, as if you *did* so, which last is a great consolation at all events.

But I more than love you and cannot cease to love you. Think of me sometimes, when the Alps and ocean divide us, but they never will, unless you wish it.

Byron

John Keats
1795–1821

John Keats is now universally regarded as one of the greatest poets in the English language, but during his lifetime the powerful, aggressive and reactionary critics of the day – those same critics who had bullied William Hazlitt – treated him as an upstart (he had trained as an apothecary and his father was a stable-keeper, which apparently disqualified him from writing poetry), and mocked his work as vulgar and over-exuberant.

All his life, Keats was short of money and surrounded by illness and death – he lost his mother, his brother and an uncle to tuberculosis before he himself fell ill with it in 1820 at the age of twenty-four. His friend Charles Brown gives a heartbreaking account of Keats's first seeing a spot of blood on his sheet: 'I know the colour of that blood; – it is arterial blood; – I cannot be deceived in that colour; – that drop of blood is my death-warrant; – I must die.' He travelled to Italy in the hope of a cure, but died there a few months later. He was buried in Rome, and on his tombstone at his request was the inscription, 'Here lies one whose name was writ on water.'

The great love of Keats's life was a Hampstead neighbour, Fanny Brawne, to whom he was engaged. His passion for Fanny often shaded into jealousy, which in turn led to her posthumous reputation as a fickle and superficial flirt, although there seems to be little evidence for this. The facts suggest that she mourned Keats throughout the 1820s, befriending his sister as he had requested. She finally married a wealthy merchant named Louis Lindo in 1833.

To Fanny Brawne, 8 July 1819

My sweet Girl,

– Your letter gave me more delight than anything in the world but yourself could do; indeed, I am almost astonished that any absent one should have the luxurious power over my senses which I feel. Even when I am not thinking of you, I perceive your tenderness and a tenderer nature stealing upon me. All my thoughts, my unhappiest days and nights, have I find not at all cured me of my love of Beauty, but made it so intense that I am miserable that you are not with me: or rather breathe in that dull sort of patience that cannot be called Life. I never knew before, what such a love as you have made me feel, was; I did not believe in it; my Fancy was afraid of it, lest it should burn me up. But if you will fully love me, though there may be some fire, 'twill not be more than we can bear when moistened and bedewed with Pleasures. You mention 'horrid people,' and ask me whether it depend upon them whether I see you again. Do understand me, my love, in this. I have so much of you in my heart that I must turn Mentor when I see a chance of harm befalling you. I would never see anything but Pleasure in your eyes, love on your lips, and Happiness in your steps. I would wish to see you among those amusements suitable to your inclinations and spirits; so that our loves might be a delight in the midst of Pleasures agreeable enough, rather than a resource from vexations and cares. But I doubt much, in case of the worst, whether I shall be philosopher enough to follow my own Lessons; if I saw my resolution give you a pain I could not. Why may I not speak of your Beauty, since without that I never could have lov'd you? I cannot conceive of any beginning of such love as I have for you but Beauty. There may be a sort of love for which, without the least sneer at it, I have the highest respect and can admire it in others; but it has not the richness, the bloom, the full form, the enchantment of love after my own heart. So let me speak of your Beauty, though to my own endangering; if you could be so cruel to me as to try elsewhere its Power. You say I am afraid I shall think you do not love me – in saying this you make me ache the more to be near you. I am at the diligent use of my faculties here, I do not pass a day without sprawling some blank verse or tagging some rhymes; and here I must confess that (since I am on that subject) I love you the more in that I believe you have liked me for my own sake and for nothing else. I have met with women whom I really think would like to be married to a Poem and to be given away by a Novel. I have seen your Comet, and only wish it was a sign that poor Rice would get well whose illness makes him rather a melancholy companion. And the more so as to conquer his feelings and hide them from me, with a forc'd Pun. I kissed your writing over in the hope you had indulged me by leaving a trace of honey. What was your dream? Tell it me and I will tell you the interpretation thereof.

   –Ever yours, my love! John Keats

To Fanny Brawne, 1820

Sweetest Fanny,
– You fear sometimes I do not love you so much as you wish? My dear Girl, I love you ever and ever and without reserve. The more I have known, the more have I lov'd. In every way, –even my jealousies have been agonies of Love; in the hottest fit I ever had I would have died for you. I have vexed you too much. But for Love! Can I help it? You are always new. The last of your kisses was ever the sweetest, the last smile the brightest; the last movement the grace-fullest. When you pass'd my window home yesterday, I was fill'd with as much admiration as if I had seen you for the first time. You uttered a half complaint once that I only lov'd your beauty. Have I nothing else then to love in you

but that? Do I not see a heart naturally furnish'd with wings imprison itself with me? No ill prospect has been able to turn your thoughts a moment from me. This perhaps should be as much a subject of sorrow as joy – but I will not talk of that. Even if you did not love me I could not help an entire devotion to you: how much more deeply then must I feel for you knowing you love me. My Mind has been the most discontented and restless one that ever was put into a body too small for it. I never felt my Mind repose upon anything with complete and undistracted enjoyment – upon no person but you. When you are in the room my thoughts never fly out of window; you always concentrate my whole senses. The anxiety shown about our Loves in your last note is an immense pleasure to me; however, you must not suffer such speculations to molest you any more; nor will I any more believe you can have the least pique against me. Brown is gone out – but here is Mrs Wylie – when she is gone I shall be awake for you. Remembrances to your mother. – Your affectionate, J. Keats

To Fanny Brawne

My dearest Girl,
– I have been a walk this morning with a book in my hand, but as usual I have been occupied with nothing but you; I wish I could say in an agreeable manner. I am tormented day and night. They talk of my going to Italy. 'Tis certain I shall never recover if I am to be so long separate from you;

yet with all this devotion to you I cannot persuade myself into any confidence of you.

Past experience connected with the fact of my long separation from you gives me agonies which are scarcely to be talked of . . .

I am literally worn to death, which seems my only recourse. I cannot forget what has pass'd. What? Nothing with a man of the world, but to me deathful. I will get rid of this as much as possible. When you were in the habit of flirting with Brown you would have left off, could your own heart have felt one half of the one pang mine did. Brown is a good sort of Man – he did not know he was doing me to death by inches. I feel the effect of every one of those hours in my side now; and for that cause though, he has done me many services, though I know his love and friendship for me, though at this moment I should be without pence were it not for his assistance, I will never see or speak to him until we are both old men, if we are to be.

I *will* resent my heart having been made a football. You will call this madness. I have heard you say that it was not unpleasant to wait a few years, you have amusements – your mind is away – you have not brooded over one idea as I have, and how should you? You are to me an object intensely desirable – the air I breathe in a room empty of you is unhealthy. I am not the same to you – no – you can wait – you have a thousand activities – you can be happy without me. Any party, anything to fill up the day has been enough.

How have you passed this month? Who have you smil'd with? All this may seem savage in me. You do not feel as I do, you do not know what it is to love, one day you may, your time is not come. Ask yourself how many unhappy hours Keats has caused you in Loneliness. For myself I have been a Martyr the whole time, and for this reason I speak; the confession is forc'd from me by the torture. I appeal to you by the blood of that Christ you believe in: Do not write to me if you have done anything this month which it would have pained me to have seen. You may have altered – if you have not – if you still behave in dancing rooms and other societies as I have seen you – I do not want to live – if you have done so I wish this coming night may be my last.

I cannot live without you, and not only you but *chaste you*, *virtuous you*. The Sun rises and sets, the day passes, and you follow the bent of your inclination to a certain extent, you have no conception of the quantity of miserable feeling that passes through me in a day.

Be serious! Love is not a plaything – and again do not write unless you can do it with a crystal conscience. I would sooner die for want of you than – Yours for ever, J. Keats

Honoré de Balzac
1799–1850

Honoré de Balzac was born in Tours. After studying law, he decided to devote his life to literature and, half-starving in a Parisian garret, he made ends meet by writing sensational novels on commission. He also became involved in several ill-advised commercial ventures in printing and publishing. In 1831, he began work on the great sequence of linked novels which became known as *La Comedie Humaine*, intended as a panoramic vision of French society; this was to occupy him for the next twenty years. Balzac's life was chaotic, his work habits eccentric, his health poor and his finances atrocious – he was unable to resist involving himself in various hare-brained money-making schemes – but *La Comedie Humaine* is regarded today as the first masterpiece of realism, and Balzac as one of the most influential writers in history.

In 1833, Balzac began a correspondence with the Countess Ewelina Hanska, who was married to a Polish landowner twenty years older than she. Their correspondence continued for seventeen years, and after the death of her husband in 1841 they travelled extensively together around Europe. They were eventually married on 15 March 1850; on 19 August of the same year, Balzac died.

To the Countess Ewelina Hanska

Oh! how I should have liked to remain half a day kneeling at your feet with my head on your lap, dreaming beautiful dreams, telling you my thoughts with languor, with rapture, sometimes not speaking at all, but pressing my lips to your gown! . . . O, my well-beloved Eva, the day of my days, the light of my nights, my hope, my adored one, my entirely beloved one, my only darling, when can I see you? Is it an illusion? Have I seen you? Ye gods! how I love your accent, just a shade thick, your mouth of kindness, of voluptuousness – allow me to say it of you, my angel of love. I am working night and day in order to go and see you for a fortnight in December. I shall pass over the Jura covered with snow; but I shall be thinking of the snowy shoulders of my love, my well-beloved. Ah! to breathe in your hair, to hold your hand, to clasp you in my arms – it is from these I get my courage! Some of my friends here are stupefied at the savage will-power I am displaying at this moment. Ah! they do not know my darling, she whose mere image robs grief of its stings. One kiss, my angel of the earth, one kiss tasted slowly, and then good-night!

I leave to-morrow, my seat is reserved, and I am going to finish my letter, because I have to put it in the post myself; my head is like an empty pumpkin, and I am in a state which disquiets me more than I can say. If I am thus in Paris, I shall have to return. I have no feeling for anything, I have no desire to live, I have no longer got the slightest energy, I seem to have no will-power left . . . I have not smiled since I left you . . .

Adieu, dear star, a thousand times blessed! There will perhaps come a moment when I shall be able to express to you the thoughts which oppress me. To-day I can only say that I love you too much for my repose, because after this August and September, I feel that I can only live near to you, and that your absence is death . . .

Adieu! I am going to take my letter to the post. A thousand tendernesses to your child a thousand times blessed; my friendly greetings to Lirette, and to you everything that is in my heart, my soul, and my brain . . . If you knew what emotion seizes me when I throw one of these packets in the box.

My soul flies towards you with these papers; I say to them like a crazy man, a thousand things; like a crazy man I think that they go towards you to repeat them to you; it is impossible for me to understand how these papers impregnated by me will be, in eleven days, in your hands, and why I remain here . . .

Oh yes, dear star, far and near, count on me like on yourself; neither I nor my devotion will fail you any more than life will fail your body. One can believe, dear fraternal soul, what one says of life at my age; well, believe me that there is no other life for me than yours. My task is done. If misfortune were to happen to you, I would go and bury myself in an obscure corner and ignored by everybody, without seeing anybody in the world; *allez*, this is not an empty word. If happiness for a woman is to know herself unique in a heart, alone, filling it in an indispensable manner, sure to shine in the intelligence of a man as his light, sure to be his blood, to animate each heart-beat, to live in his thought as the substance itself of that thought, and having the certainty that it would be always and always so; *eh bien*, dear sovereign of my soul, you can call yourself happy, and happy *senza brama*, for so I shall be for you till death. One can feel satiety for human things, there is none for divine things, and this word alone can explain what you are for me.

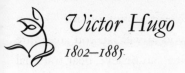

Victor Hugo
1802–1885

It is almost impossible to describe Victor Hugo without falling back on the word 'colossus'. He lived through most of a turbulent century in France, was exiled by Napoleon III for twenty years, and was, variously, a poet, a playwright, an essayist, a novelist, a painter and a politician. He was a monarchist who turned socialist, an aristocrat who became a champion of the poor.

Hugo was born of conflict. His father was an atheist republican and high-ranking officer in Napoleon's army; his mother a Catholic royalist. His parents were separated when he was small, and he lived for the most part with his mother. Adèle Foucher was a childhood friend with whom he fell in love, but his mother deemed the match unsuitable. It wasn't until after her death that he felt free to marry Adèle in 1822. Hugo was at that time primarily a poet, whose work received great acclaim. Hugo and Adèle had five children, but were not faithful to each other; in 1831, Adèle had an affair with the critic Saint-Beuve; in 1833, Hugo fell in love with Juliette Drouet, an actress, who for the next fifty years was his mistress, secretary and travelling companion; she died in 1882.

Victor Hugo's best-known works outside France are probably *Notre Dame de Paris* (1832) and *Les Misérables* (seventeen years in the writing, published in 1862). When he died, three million mourners followed his cortège to the Pantheon in Paris, where he was buried among France's greatest men.

To Adèle Foucher, January 1820

A few words from you, my beloved Adèle, have again changed the state of my mind. Yes, you can do anything with me, and tomorrow, I should be dead indeed if the gentle sound of your voice, the tender pressure of your adored lips, do not suffice to recall the life to my body. With what different feelings to yesterday's I shall lay myself down tonight! Yesterday, Adèle, I no longer believed in your love; the hour of death would have been welcome to me.

And yet I still said to myself, 'if it be true that she does not love me, if nothing in me could deserve the blessing of her love, without which there is no longer any charm in life, is that a reason for dying? Do I exist for my own personal happiness? No; my whole existence is devoted to her, even in spite of her. And by what right should I have dared to aspire to her love? Am I, then, more than an angel or a deity? I love her, true, even I; I am ready to sacrifice everything gladly for her sake – everything, even the hope of being loved by her; there is no devotedness of which I am not capable for her, for one of her smiles, for one of her looks. But could I be otherwise? Is she not the sole aim of my life? That she may show indifference to me, even hate, will be my misfortune, that is all. What does it matter, so that it does not injure her happiness? Yes, if she cannot love me I ought to blame myself only. My duty is to keep close to her steps, to surround her existence with mine, to serve her as a barrier against all dangers, to offer her my head as a stepping-stone, to place myself unceasingly between her and all sorrows, without claiming any reward, without expecting any recompense. Only too happy if she deign sometimes to cast a pitying look upon her slave, and to remember him in the hour of danger! Alas! if she only allow me to give my life to anticipate her every desire, all her caprices; if she but permit me to kiss with respect her adored footprints; if she but consent to lean upon me at times amidst the difficulties of life: Then I shall have obtained the only happiness to which I have the presumption to aspire. Because I am ready to sacrifice all for her, does she owe me any gratitude? Is it her fault that I love her? Must she, on that account, believe herself constrained to love me? No! she may sport with my devotion, repay my services with hate, and repulse my idolatry with scorn, without my having for a moment the right to complain of that angel; nor ought I to cease for an instant to lavish upon her all that which she would disdain. And should every one of my days have been marked by some sacrifice for her, I should still, at the day of my death, have discharged nothing of the infinite debt that my existence owes to hers.'

Such, my well-beloved Adèle, were the thoughts and resolutions of my mind at this time yesterday. Today they are still the same. Only there is mingled with them the certainty of happiness – such great happiness that I cannot think of it without trembling, and scarcely dare to believe in it.

Then it is true that you love me, Adèle? Tell me, can I trust in this enchanting idea? Don't you think that I shall end by becoming insane with joy if ever I can pass the whole of my life at your feet, sure of making you as happy as I shall be myself, sure of being adored by you as you are adored by me? Oh! your letter has restored peace to me, your words this evening have filled me with happiness. A thousand thanks, Adèle, my well-beloved angel. Would that I could prostrate myself before you as before a divinity. How happy you make me! Adieu, adieu, I shall pass a very happy night, dreaming of you.

Sleep well, and allow your husband to take the twelve kisses which you promised him, besides all those yet unpromised.

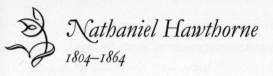

Nathaniel Hawthorne
1804–1864

Nathaniel Hawthorne was born in Salem, Massachusetts. A forebear, John Hathorne, was one of the judges who oversaw the Salem witch trials; Hawthorne might have added the 'w' to his surname to rid himself of this association. He was educated at Bowdoin College, and in 1837 went to work at the Boston Custom House. In 1842, he married Sophia Peabody, a painter, illustrator and member of the American Transcendentalist movement, whose members included Bronson Alcott, the father of Louisa May Alcott, the author of *Little Women*. After their marriage, the Hawthornes settled in Concord, Massachusetts, at the Old Manse, where they seem to have been very happy. In 1850, Hawthorne published his most famous novel, *The Scarlet Letter*, an immediate bestseller.

Four years after Nathaniel's death, Sophia moved to England; the family had lived there for four years between 1853 and 1857, when Nathaniel had been appointed United States Consul in Liverpool. She died in 1871, and was buried in Kensal Green Cemetery in London. In 2006, her remains were removed to the Hawthorne family plot in Concord, where she now lies next to her husband.

The most striking feature of this letter to Sophia, aside from the vast affection it conveys, is its immediacy; the voice is like that of a friend recounting a recent dream.

To Sophia

Unspeakably Belovedest,
– Thy letter has just been handed to me. It was most comfortable to me, because it gives such a picture of thy life with the children. I could see the whole family of my heart before my eyes, and could hear you all talking together . . .

The other night, I dreamt that I was at Newton, in a room with thee and with several people; and thou tookst occasion to announce that thou hadst now ceased to be my wife, and hadst taken another husband. Thou madest this intelligence known with such perfect composure and sang froid, – not particularly addressing me, but the company generally, – that it benumbed my thoughts and feelings, so that I had nothing to say. But, hereupon, some woman who was there present, informed the company that, in this state of affairs, having ceased to be thy husband, I had become hers, and, turning to me, very coolly inquired whether she or I should write to inform my mother of the new arrangement! How the children were to be divided, I know not.

I only know that my heart suddenly broke loose, and I began to expostulate with thee in an infinite agony, in the midst of which I awoke. But the sense of unspeakable injury and outrage hung about me for a long time, and even yet it has not quite departed. Thou shouldst not behave so when thou comest to me in dreams.

Oh, Phoebe, I want thee much. Thou art the only person in the world that ever was necessary to me. Other people have occasionally been more or less agreeable; but I think I was always more at ease alone than in anybody's company, till I knew thee. And now I am only myself when thou art within my reach. Thou art an unspeakably beloved woman. How couldst thou inflict such frozen agony upon me in that dream?

If I write any more, it would only be to express more lovings and longings; and as they are impossible to express, I may as well close.

Thy Husband

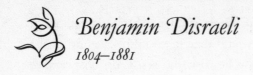

Benjamin Disraeli
1804–1881

Benjamin Disraeli, novelist and prime minister, grew up in London; his father was a literary man of independent means. The family converted from Judaism to Christianity in 1817. Disraeli initially studied as a lawyer, but gave it up to become a writer. He adopted a somewhat startling mode of dress (velvet trousers, patterned waistcoats, etc.), travelled around Europe and the Ottoman Empire, and wrote a number of novels with little success, one of which – a satire on London society – managed to offend several of his patrons. He also accrued huge debts.

In the 1830s, Disraeli turned to politics, and in 1837 became an MP. He also began courting Mary Anne Wyndham Lewis, the widow of one of his political sponsors. She was twelve years older than he, and her large income and London property were undoubtedly an attraction for Disraeli, but she was no fool, and as the letter below illustrates, she took some persuading as to the sincerity of his motives. She was eventually convinced, and they were married in August 1839.

Mary Anne – tiny, talkative, garishly dressed – was mocked as not quite the thing by smart society, but she was an enormous help to Disraeli; she methodically and generously managed his horrific debts ('Dizzy' was of the 'pretend-it-isn't-happening-and-pay-a-ruinous-rate-of-interest' school of financial management), and was a talented political campaigner and source of unstinting practical support. Once, Disraeli, returning home late after a political triumph, found her waiting up for him with a bottle of champagne and exclaimed, 'Why, my dear, you are more like a mistress than a wife!', which, while not the most tactful or romantic of compliments, should be seen in the light of the fact that Mary Anne was seventy-five at the time, and the two had been married for nearly thirty years. Disraeli was heartbroken when she died in 1872.

To Mary Anne Wyndham Lewis,
Sent from Park Street, Thursday night, 7 February 1839

I wd have endeavoured to have spoken to you of that which it was necessary you shd know, & I wished to have spoken with the calmness which was natural to one humiliated & distressed. I succeeded so far as to be considered a 'selfish bully' & to be desired to quit your house for ever. I have recourse therefore to this miserable method of communicating with you; none can be more imperfect but I write as if it were the night before my execution.

Every hour of my life I hear of an approaching union from all lips except your own. At last a friend anxious to distinguish me by some unusual mark of his favour & thinking to confer on me a distinction of which I shd be proud, offers me one of his seats for our happy month. The affair was then approaching absurdity. There was a period, & a much earlier one, when similar allusions to the future & intimations of what must occur were frequent from your lips; as if you thought some daily hint of the impending result was necessary to stimulate or to secure my affection.

As a woman of the world, which you are thoroughly, you ought not, you cannot be, unacquainted with the difference that subsists between our relative positions. The continuance of the present state of affairs cd only render you disreputable; me it wd render infamous. There is only one construction which Society, & justly, puts upon a connection between a woman who is supposed to be rich & a man whom she avowedly loves & does not marry. In England especially there is no stigma more damning; it is one which no subsequent conduct or position ever permits to be forgotten. It has crushed men who have committed with impunity even crimes; some things may indeed be more injurious; none more ignominious.

This reputation impends over me. I will at least preserve that honor which is the breath of my existence. At present I am in the position of an insolvent whose credit is not suspected; but ere a few weeks I must inevitably chuse between being ridiculous or being contemptible; I must be recognised as being jilted, or I must at once sink into what your friend Lady Morgan has already styled me 'Mrs Wyndham Lewis's De Novo'.

This leads me to the most delicat of subjects, but in justice to us both I will write with the utmost candor. I avow, when I first made my advances to you I was influenced by no romantic feelings. My father had long wished me to marry; my settling in life was the implied tho' not stipulated, condition of a disposition of his property, which wd have been convenient to me. I myself, about to commence a practical career, wished for the solace of a home, & shrunk from all the torturing passions of intrigue. I was not blind to worldly advantages in such an alliance, but I had already proved that my heart was not to be purchased. I found you in sorry, & that heart was touched. I found you, as I thought, aimiable, tender, & yet acute & gifted with no ordinary mind – one whom I cd look upon with pride as the partner of my life, who cd sympathise with all my projects & feelings, console me in the moments of depression, share my hour of triumph, & work with me for our honor and happiness.

Now for your fortune: I write the sheer truth. That fortune proved to be much less than I, or the world, imagined. It was in fact, as far as I was concerned, a fortune which cd not benefit me in the slightest degree; it was merely a jointure not greater than your station required; enough to maintain your establishment & gratify your private tastes. To eat & to sleep in that house & nominally to call it mine – these cd be only objects for a penniless adventurer. Was this an inducement for me to sacrifice my sweet liberty, & that indefinite future wh: is one of the charms of existence? No, when months ago I told you there was only one link between us, I felt that my heart was inextricably engaged to you, & but for that I wd have terminated our acquaintance. From that moment I devoted to you all the passion of my being. Alas! It has been poured upon the sand.

As time progressed I perceived in your character & mine own certain qualities, wh: convinced me that if I wished to persevere that profound & unpolluted affection wh: subsisted between us money must never be introduced. Had we married, not one shilling of your income shd ever have been seen by me; neither indirectly nor directly, wd I have interfered in the management of your affairs. If Society justly stigmatizes with infamy the hired lover, I shrink with equal disgust from being the paid husband.

You have branded me as selfish – Alas! I fear you have apparent cause. I confess it with the most heart rending humiliation. Little did I think when I wept, when in a manner so unexpected & so irresistible you poured upon my bosom the treasured savings of your affection, that I received the wages of my degradation! Weak, wretched fool! This led to my accepting your assistance in my trial; but that was stipulated to be a loan & I only waited for the bill which my agent gave me when you were at Bradenhaim as the balance of our accounts & which becomes due this very month, to repay it into yr bankers.

By heavens as far as worldly interests are concerned, your alliance cd not benefit me. All that society can offer is at my command; it is not the apparent possession of a jointure that ever elevates position. I can live, as I live, without disgrace, until the inevitable progress of events gives me that independence which is all I require. I have entered into these ungracious details because you reproached me with my interested views. No; I wd not condescend to be the minion of a princess; and not all the gold of Ophir shd ever lead me to the altar. Far different are the qualities which I require in the sweet participator of my existence. My nature demands that my life shall be perpetual love.

Upon your general conduct to me I make no comment. It is now useless. I will not upbraid you. I will only blame myself. All warned me: public and private – all were eager to save me from the perdition into which I have fallen. Coxcomb to suppose that you wd conduct yourself to me in a manner different to that in which you have behaved to fifty others!

And yet I thought I had touched your heart! Wretched Idiot!

As a woman of the world you must have foreseen this. And for the gratification of your vanity, for the amusement of ten months, for the diversion of your seclusion, could you find the heart to do this? Was there no ignoble prey at hand that you must degrade a bird of heaven? Why not have let your Captain Neil have been the minion of your gruesome hours with humiliating & debasing me. Nature never intended me for a toy & dupe. But you have struck deep. You have done that which my enemies have yet failed to do: you have broken my spirit. From the highest to the humblest scene of my life, from the brilliant world of fame to my own domestic hearth, you have poisoned all. I have no place of refuge: home is odious, the world oppressive.

Triumph – I seek not to conceal my state. It is not sorrow, it is not wretchedness; it is anguish, it is the *endurance* of that pang which is the passing characteristic of agony. All that can prostrate a man has fallen on my victim head. My heart outraged, my pride wounded, my honor nearly tainted. I know well that ere a few days can pass I shall be scoff & jest of that world, to gain whose admiration has been the effort of my life. I have only one source of solace – the consciousness of self-respect. Will that uphold me? A terrible problem that must quickly be solved.

Farewell. I will not affect to wish you happiness for it is not in your nature to obtain it. For a few years you may flutter in some frivolous circle. But the time will come when you will sigh for any heart that could be fond and despair of one that can be faithful. Then will be the penal hour of retribution; then you will recall to your memory the passionate heart that you have forfeited, and the genius you have betrayed.

D.

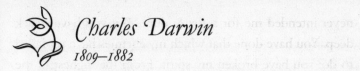

Charles Darwin
1809–1882

The single most important event of Charles Darwin's life came in 1831, when he was given the chance to travel to 'Terra del Fuego and home by the East Indies' aboard the *Beagle*, a surveying ship. The invitation was down to sheer luck – he certainly had no qualifications as a naturalist, having spent most of his time at university drinking, riding and gambling. The voyage changed him for ever. He left England an aimless young man, and returned five years later a scientist, whose observations would change the world.

By 1838, he decided it was time to be married – after drawing up a document in two columns, headed respectively 'marry' and 'not marry', like the great cataloguer he was. Under 'marry', he wrote, 'Constant companion . . . object to be beloved and played with . . . better than a dog anyhow . . . Only picture to yourself a nice soft wife on a sofa with good fire, & books & music'. The advantages elucidated in the 'not marry' column included 'conversation of clever men at clubs – not forced to visit relatives, & to bend in every trifle'. He became engaged to Emma

Wedgwood, a first cousin; the wedding took place in January 1839. They settled in London briefly – the letter here shows Darwin's excitement as he looked around the house where they were to live, presumably picturing 'a nice soft wife on a sofa' – and then moved to Down House in Kent, where they lived for the rest of their lives.

The marriage was a happy one, although the devout Emma feared for the effects of her husband's scientific discoveries on the fate of his immortal soul. Darwin's health was not good, and he worried about it constantly, as well as worrying about Emma's being upset by outraged criticism of his work; there is speculation that he delayed publishing his theory of evolution out of respect for her religiosity. They had ten children (three of whom died young), and despite his health concerns, Darwin lived to seventy-two. He is buried in Westminster Abbey, close to the monument to Isaac Newton. Emma died in 1896 and is buried in the churchyard at Downe.

To Emma Wedgwood
Sunday Night. Athenaeum. 20 January 1839

... I cannot tell you how much I enjoyed my Maer visit, – I

felt in anticipation my future tranquil life: how I do hope you may be as happy as I know I shall be: but it frightens me, as often as I think of what a family you have been one of. I was thinking this morning how it came, that I, who am fond of talking and am scarcely ever out of spirits, should so entirely rest my notions of happiness on quietness, and a good deal of solitude: but I believe the explanation is very simple and I mention it because it will give you hopes, that I shall gradually grow less of a brute, it is that during the five years of my voyage (and indeed I may add these two last) which from the active manner in which they have been passed, may be said to be the commencement of my real life, the whole of my pleasure was derived from what passed in my mind, while admiring views by myself, travelling across the wild deserts or glorious forests or pacing the deck of the poor little 'Beagle' at night. Excuse this much egotism, –I give it you because I think you will humanize me, and soon teach me there is greater happiness than building theories and accumulating facts in silence and solitude. My own dearest Emma, I earnestly pray, you may never regret the great, and I will add very good, deed, you are to perform on the Tuesday: my own dear future wife, God bless you . . .

The Lyells called on me to-day after church; as Lyell was so full of geology he was obliged to disgorge, –and I dine there on Tuesday for an especial confidence. I was quite ashamed of myself to-day, for we talked for half an hour, unsophisticated geology, with poor Mrs Lyell sitting by, a monument of patience. I want practice in ill-treatment of the female sex, –I did not observe Lyell had any compunction; I hope to harden my conscience in time: few husbands seem to find it difficult to effect this. Since my return I have taken several looks, as you will readily believe, into the drawing-room; I suppose my taste [for] harmonious colours is already deteriorated, for I declare the room begins to look less ugly. I take so much pleasure in the house, I declare I am just like a great overgrown child with a new toy; but then, not like a real child, I long to have a co-partner and possessor.

Alfred de Musset
1810–1857

Alfred de Musset was born in Paris to a well-to-do literary family. A novelist, playwright and poet, he enjoyed great success before he was twenty.

In 1833, having read her second novel, Alfred de Musset wrote a letter to George Sand (the pseudonym of Amandine Aurore Lucile Dupin); they met, and he fell in love with her. She had left her husband, the Baron Casimir Dudevant, two years earlier. De Musset was twenty-three, and Sand twenty-nine.

George Sand had a burgeoning reputation as an editor and a novelist. Her cross-dressing and her male *nom-de-plume* had led people to make the predictable sneers about her sexuality and personal life, and her feminist and socialist principles meant that she constantly attracted criticism, but the number of people who fell in love with her suggests that she was a very charismatic woman.

In the letter here, Alfred de Musset declares himself for the first time, claiming that he has no hope of her returning his affection, and referring ruefully to a trip to Italy they had planned which he now assumes, in the light of his declaration, will have to be cancelled.

In fact, they became lovers and they did go to Italy together; the trip was an absolute disaster, and their relationship did not survive much longer.

De Musset died at the age of forty-seven; George Sand at the age of seventy-two, after an eventful life that contained many more adventures and love affairs.

To George Sand, 1833

My dear George,
– I have something stupid and ridiculous to tell you. I am foolishly writing you instead of having told you this, I do not know why, when returning from that walk. To-night I shall be annoyed at having done so. You will laugh in my face, will take me for a maker of phrases in all my relations with you hitherto. You will show me the door and you will think I am lying. I am in love with you. I have been thus since the first day I called on you. I thought I should cure myself in seeing you quite simply as a friend. There are many things in your character which could cure me; I have tried to convince myself of that as much as I could. But I pay too dearly for the moments I pass with you. I prefer to tell you and I have done well, because I shall suffer much less if I am cured by your showing me the door now. This night during which . . . [George Sand, who edited de Musset's letters for publication, crossed out the last two words,

and with scissors cut out the following line] I had decided to let you know that I was out of town, but I do not want to make a mystery of it nor have the appearance of quarrelling without a reason. Now George, you will say: 'Another fellow, who is about to become a nuisance,' as you say. If I am not quite the firstcomer for you, tell me, as you would have told me yesterday in speaking of somebody else, what I ought to do. But I beg of you, if you intend to say that you doubt the truth of what I am writing, then I had rather you did not answer me at all. I know how you think of me, and I have nothing to hope for in telling you this. I can only foresee losing a friend and the only agreeable hours I have passed for a month. But I know that you are kind, that you have loved, and I put my trust in you, not as a mistress, but as a frank and loyal comrade. George, I am an idiot to deprive myself of the pleasure of seeing you the short time you have still to spend in Paris, before your departure for Italy, where we would have spent such beautiful nights together, if I had the strength. But the truth is that I suffer, and that my strength is wanting.

Alfred de Musset

Robert Schumann
1810–1856

Robert Schumann studied law at Leipzig and Heidelberg, but his real love was music. His piano teacher was Friedrich Wieck, whose daughter Clara, nine years younger than Robert, was already a talented pianist. Robert too was gifted, but an injury to his hand meant a career as a musician became impossible, and so he turned his attention to composition and criticism, founding an influential journal in which he championed new composers.

Robert and Clara fell in love when Clara was fifteen, and in 1837, Robert asked her father's permission for them to marry, which he withheld – Robert gives an account of the dreadful interview in the second letter below. For three years, the lovers battled for Friedrich's consent, going to court in the process; he never gave it, and so Robert and Clara were eventually married without it in 1840, the same year in which Robert composed many of his famous *Lieder*. Acclaim for Clara grew throughout Europe, and she showcased many of her husband's compositions, although he did not receive the same level of recognition as his wife.

Robert first experienced symptoms of mental illness in 1844, suffering from depression and delusions, but he had recovered by the following year. Ten years later, the symptoms returned, and he attempted suicide by throwing himself into the Rhine; he was rescued, but spent the remaining two years of his life in an asylum. Clara lived for another forty years.

To Clara Wieck, Leipzig, 1834

My dear and revered Clara,

– There are haters of beauty, who maintain that swans were really geese of a larger kind – one might say with equal justification that distance is only a close-up that has been pushed apart. And so indeed it is, for I speak with you daily (yes, even more softly than I usually do), and yet I know that you understand me. In the beginning I had various plans with regard to our correspondence. I wanted, for instance, to start a public one with you in the music journal; then I wanted to fill my air-balloon (you know that I own one) with ideas for letters, and arrange an ascent in a favourable wind with a suitable destination . . . I wanted to catch butterflies as letter-carriers to you. I wanted to send my letters first to Paris, so that you should open them with great curiosity, and then, more than surprised, would believe me in Paris. In short, I had many witty dreams in my head, from which only to-day the horn of the postilion [postman] has awakened me. Postilions, my dear Clara, have, by the way, as magical an effect on me as the most excellent champagne. One seems to have no head, one has such a delightfully light heart, when one hears them trumpeting so joyously out into the world. They are real waltzes of yearning to me, these trumpet-blasts, which remind us of something that we do not possess. As I said, the postilion blew me out of my old dreams into new ones . . .

To Clara, on her father's opposition to their marriage,
18 September 1837

– The interview with your father was terrible . . . Such frigidness, such disingenuousness, such deviousness, such contradictions – he has a new manner of destruction, he stabs you to the heart with the handle of the knife . . .

What now then, my dear Clara? I do not know what to do now – *not in the slightest*. My wits are going to pieces here, and in such a frame of mind one can assuredly not come to terms with your father. What now then, what now then? Above all, prepare yourself, and do *not once allow yourself to be sold* . . . I trust you, oh, *from all my heart*, and that is what upholds me . . . But you will have to be very *strong*, more than you dream of. Did not your father say those terrible words to me, that nothing can move *him*; he will *compel you by force*, if he fails in stratagem. Be afraid of everything!

I am to-day so dead, so *humiliated*, that I can hardly conceive a beautiful, good idea. So dishearted as to give you up I have not yet become; but so embittered, so hurt in my holiest feelings, so locked in a frame of the most ordinary commonplace.

If I only had a word from you! You must tell me what I am to do. Otherwise my being will turn to scorn and a byword, and I shall be off and away.

Not even to be allowed to see you! We could do so, he said, but in a neutral spot, in the presence of all, a regular show for everybody. How chilling all that is — how it rankles! We might even correspond, when you are on a journey! — that was all that he would consent to . . .

Give me consolation, dear God, that he may not let me perish in despair. I am torn up by the roots of my life.

Robert Browning
1812–1889

Elizabeth Barrett was a poet of some standing when Robert Browning, six years her junior, first wrote to her on 10 January 1845; it was a fan letter, but prefigured the many love letters that were to follow: 'I love your verses with all my heart, dear Miss Barrett.' Elizabeth was an invalid, and lived with her brothers and sisters and tyrannical father in Wimpole Street, London. Robert and Elizabeth met for the first time on 20 May 1845; shortly afterwards Robert rashly declared that he had fallen in love with her. Elizabeth, alarmed, withdrew somewhat; the two rebuilt their relationship on the basis of friendship. The turning-point came in the autumn of that year, when Elizabeth was advised to spend the winter in Italy for the sake of her health; her father refused to let her go, and Browning declared that he would marry her immediately to free her from her father's grasp. This time, Elizabeth was receptive, and they spent almost a year planning their escape, particularly the financial practicalities, as Elizabeth was sure that she would be disinherited by her father – which she was.

Robert and Elizabeth were married in secret at the

parish church of St Marylebone on 12 September 1846, and left immediately for Italy. Elizabeth gave birth to a son in 1849 at the age of forty-three. Her health was never good – there was no miraculous recovery, and she used opiates all her life – and there was no reconciliation with her father, despite her many efforts, but the couple were happy and productive; it was during her marriage that Elizabeth produced perhaps her greatest work, *Aurora Leigh*. They divided their time between Italy, France and London, until Elizabeth's death in Florence in 1861. Robert Browning lived another twenty-eight years, but never remarried, declaring that his heart was buried in Florence. He died in Italy; his body was returned to England, and he is buried in Poets' Corner in Westminster Abbey.

To Elizabeth Barrett:
Wednesday [postmarked 28 January 1846]

Ever dearest,
– I will say, as you desire, nothing on that subject – but this strictly for myself: you engaged me to consult my own good in the keeping or breaking our engagement; not *your* good as it might even seem to me; much less seem to another. My only good in this world – that against which all the world

goes for nothing – is to spend my life with you, and be yours. You know that when I *claim* anything, it is really yourself in me – you *give* me a right and bid me use it, and I, in fact, am most obeying you when I appear most exacting on my own account – so, in that feeling, I dare claim, once for all, and in all possible cases (except that dreadful one of your becoming worse again . . . in which case I wait till life ends with both of us), I claim your promise's fulfilment – say, at the summer's end: it cannot be for your good that this state of things should continue. We can go to Italy for a year or two and be happy as day and night are long. For me, I adore you. This is all unnecessary, I feel as I write: but you will think of the main fact as *ordained*, granted by God, will you not, dearest? – so, not to be put in doubt *ever again* – then, we can go quietly thinking of after matters. Till tomorrow, and ever after, God bless my heart's own, own Ba. All my soul follows you, love – encircles you – and I live in being yours.

To Elizabeth Barrett on the morning of their wedding day,
12 September 1846

You will only expect a few words. What will those be? When the heart is full it may run over; but the real fullness stays within . . . Words can never tell you . . . how perfectly dear you are to me – perfectly dear to my heart and soul. I look back and in every one point, every word and gesture, every letter, every *silence* – you have been entirely perfect to me –

I would not change one word, one look. My hope and aim are to preserve this love, not to fall from it – for which I trust to God, who procured it for me, and doubtless can preserve it. Enough now, my dearest own Ba! You have given me the highest, completest proof of love that ever one human being gave another. I am all gratitude – and all pride . . . that my life has been so crowned by you.

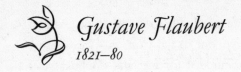

Gustave Flaubert
1821–80

The great novelist Gustave Flaubert is best known for *Madame Bovary*, his forensic examination of adultery, which led to his being prosecuted (unsuccessfully) for immorality. Arguably his most important female relationship was with his mother; Flaubert lived with her outside Rouen at Croisset on the Seine for much of his adult life. His one serious love affair was with Louise Colet, a prolific writer of poems, novels, essays and journalism, and a dazzling beauty who presided over a renowned Parisian *salon* and was confidante to many of the great writers of the age. He called her his 'Muse'; their relationship lasted from 1846–1854, but ended badly, and Colet later published a fictional account of it in her novel *Lui*. Flaubert also had a close relationship with George Sand.

Flaubert died at the age of fifty-nine of a stroke; his health had never been good, and he suffered from both syphilis and 'nervous fits', probably epilepsy. Louise Colet died in 1876.

To Louise Colet
Croisset, night of Saturday, 1 o'clock

You say to me very tender things, dear Muse. *Eh bien*, receive in exchange all those still more tender things than you could imagine. Your love ends by penetrating me like a lukewarm rain, and I feel myself soaked in it down to the very bottom of my heart. Hast thou not everything needful for me to love thee – body, mind, tenderness? You are simple of soul and strong of head, very little poetical, and extremely a poet; there is nothing but good in you, and you are entirely like your bosom, white and soft to the touch. Those I have known *va*, were not equal to you, and I doubt whether those that I have desired were your equal. I try sometimes to imagine to myself your face when you are old, and it seems to me that I shall love you as much, perhaps more.

To George Sand, 1866
Monday night

You are sad, poor friend and dear master; it was you of whom I thought on learning of Duveyrier's death. Since you loved him, I am sorry for you. That loss is added to others. How we keep these dead souls in our hearts. Each one of us carries within himself his necropolis.

I am entirely UNDONE since your departure; it seems to me as if I had not seen you for ten years. My one subject of conversation with my mother is you, everyone here loves you. Under what star were you born, pray, to unite in your person such diverse qualities, so numerous and so rare?

I don't know what sort of feeling I have for you, but I have a particular tenderness for you, and one I have never felt for anyone, up to now. We understood each other, didn't we, that was good.

I especially missed you last evening at ten o'clock. There was a fire at my wood-seller's. The sky was rose color and the Seine the color of gooseberry sirup. I worked at the engine for three hours and I came home as worn out as the Turk with the giraffe.

A newspaper in Rouen, the *Nouvelliste*, told of your visit to Rouen, so that Saturday after leaving you I met several bourgeois indignant at me for not exhibiting you. The best thing was said to me by a former sub-prefect: 'Ah! if we had known that she was here . . . we would have we would have . . . ' he hunted five minutes for the word; 'we would have smiled for her.' That would have been very little, would it not?

To 'love you more' is hard for me – but I embrace you tenderly. Your letter of this morning, so melancholy, reached the BOTTOM of my heart. We separated at the moment when many things were on the point of coming to our lips. All the doors between us two are not yet open. You inspire me with a great respect and I do not dare to question you.

Walter Bagehot
1826–1877

Walter Bagehot was a journalist, political commentator and economist, now most famous for his writings on the monarchy; he came from a prominent banking family in Somerset. Bagehot was very close to his mother, who was beautiful, affectionate and witty, but who had seen three of her five children die and was afflicted by psychotic episodes which cast a shadow over his childhood. He was encouraged in intellectual pursuits by his father, who had an extensive library.

A brilliant scholar, Bagehot took an MA from University College, London; he worked first as a lawyer, which he hated, and then as a banker, which he didn't really like any better, asserting that 'sums are a matter of opinion'. But his work at the bank in Bristol left him plenty of time for journalism. He founded a magazine, and from there graduated to editing the *Economist*, writing on a variety of political, economic and literary matters. In 1857, he became engaged to Eliza Wilson, the daughter of the *Economist*'s proprietor; they married in 1858 and settled in Somerset.

This charming letter, written during their engagement, attests to their initially passionate and happy relationship, but that state of affairs did not last. Bagehot was extraordinarily prolific, always up against a deadline, very sociable and fond of metropolitan life; Eliza could not share in his work or his enthusiasms, and grew increasingly withdrawn. They had no children.

To Elizabeth Wilson
Herd's Hill, 22 November 1857

My dearest Eliza,
I fear you will think the answer I wrote yesterday to your most kind and *delicious* letter, was very superficial, but I wrote it at once while people were talking and bothering me. I have now read yours over and over more times than I should like to admit. I awoke in the middle of the night and immediately lit a candle to read it a few times again. It has given me more pleasure than I ever received from a letter, and infinitely more than I thought it possible I could receive from one. I fancy that it is not now an effort to you to write to me – at least it reads as though it was written without effort. Yet it tells me things which with your deep and reserved nature it must have cost you much to put on paper. I wish indeed I could feel worthy of your affection – my reason, if not my imagination, is getting to believe you when you whisper to me that I have it, but as somebody says in Miss Austen, 'I do not at all mind having what is too good

for me'; my delight is at times intense. You must not suppose because I tell you of the wild, burning pain which I have felt, and at times, though I am and *ought* to be much soothed, still feel, that my love for you has ever been mere suffering. Even at the worst there was a wild, delicious excitement which I would not have lost for the world. At first, and before the feeling was very great it was simple pleasure to me to come to Claverton, and the charm of our early intellectual talks was very great, although of late, and particularly since the day in the conservatory, the feeling has been too eager not to have a good deal of pain in it, and the tension of mind has really been very great at times, still the time that I have known and loved you is immensely the happiest I have ever known. My spirits always make me cheerful in a superficial way, but they do not *satisfy*, and somehow life even before I was engaged to you was sweeter and gentler, and the jars and jangles of action lost their influence, and literature had a new value since *you* liked my writing, and everything has had a gloss upon it. Though I have come to Claverton the last few times with the notion that the gloss would go – that I should burst out and you would be tranquil and kind and considerate and *refuse* and I should never see you again. I had a vision of the thing which I keep by me. As it has *not* happened I am afraid this is egotistical – indeed I know it is – but I am not sure that egotism is bad in letters, and if I write to you I *must* write about what I feel for you. It is odd how completely our feelings change. No one can tell the effort it was to me to tell you I loved you – why I do not know, but it made me gasp for breath, and now it is absolutely pleasure to me to tell it to you and bore you with it in every form, and I should like to write it in big letters I LOVE YOU all across the page by way of emphasis. I know you will think me very childish and be shaken in your early notion that I am intellectual, but I cannot help it. This is my state of mind.

To change the subject, what is the particular advantage of being rubbed at *Edinburgh*? Since yesterday I have made careful enquiries and am assured that the English can rub. Why not be rubbed in Somersetshire? Let the doctor mark the place and have a patch put to show where and let any able-bodied party in the West of England rub on the *same* place and surely it will be as well? Does the man's touch do good to disease like the King's?

By incredible researches in an old box I have found the poem I mentioned to you. I wish I had not, for I thought it was better. I have not seen it for several years and it is not so good as I fancied – perhaps not good at all – but I think you may care to read it and you can't read it unless I send it and therefore I do send it. The young lady's name is Orithyia. The Greek legend is that she was carried away by the north wind. I have chosen to believe that she was in love with the north wind, but I am not aware that she ever declared her feelings explicitly in any document. By the way, you have. I have just read your letter in that light and I go about murmuring, 'I have made that dignified girl *commit* herself, I have, I have', and then I vault over the sofa with exultation. Those are the feelings of the person you have connected yourself with. *Please* don't be offended at my rubbish. Sauciness is my particular line. I am always rude to everybody I respect. I could write to you of the deep and serious feelings which I hope you believe really are in my heart, but my pen jests of itself and always will.

Yours with the fondest and deepest love,
Walter Bagehot

Mark Twain
1835–1910

Samuel Langhorne Clemens (Mark Twain), renowned American writer, lecturer and satirist, grew up in Hannibal, a Missouri port town on the Mississippi, the river that provided him with inspiration all his life. At fourteen, Clemens began working as a printer's apprentice, and also started writing his first pieces of journalism. He moved around the country a great deal, educating himself in libraries and working for various printers and publishers; at the age of twenty-two, he was inspired to become a steamboat pilot on the Mississippi, a dangerous and highly skilled occupation.

In 1868, Clemens fell in love with Olivia ('Livy') Langdon, the daughter of a family of wealthy liberals in upstate New York; her parents had been 'conductors' on the Underground Railroad for fugitive slaves. They were married in 1870.

Clemens was a very prolific and extremely success-ful writer of journalism, travel books and novels (*Tom Sawyer*, probably his most famous work, appeared in 1876), and travelled constantly on lecture tours around the US and Europe – he was enormously popular in the UK. On one of these tours, he met Charles Darwin, who was a huge admirer. Clemens was also an enthusiastic inventor; he registered several patents and poured hundreds of thousands of dollars into the development of the Paige typewriter, which astounded all who saw it but which never actually worked properly. He earned a good living but was hopeless with money, at one point declaring himself bankrupt.

He and Livy were very happily married and had four children; tragically, their first son died as a baby, and two of his daughters died in their twenties. Livy herself died in 1904, leaving her husband bereft.

To Livy on her thirtieth birthday
HARTFORD, *27 November 1875*

Livy darling,

Six years have gone by since I made my first great success in life and won you, and thirty years have passed since Providence made preparation for that happy success by sending you into the world. Every day we live together adds to the security of my confidence, that we can never any more wish to be separated than that we can ever imagine a regret that we were ever joined. You are dearer to me to-day, my child, than you were upon the last anniversary of this birth-day;

you were dearer then than you were a year before – you have grown more and more dear from the first of those anniversaries, and I do not doubt that this precious progression will continue on to the end.

Let us look forward to the coming anniversaries, with their age and their gray hairs without fear and without depression, trusting and believing that the love we bear each other will be sufficient to make them blessed.

So, with abounding affection for you and our babies, I hail this day that brings you the matronly grace and dignity of three decades!

Always Yours

S. L. C.

ST. NICHOLAS, *Aug. 26th, '78.*

Livy darling,

We came through a-whooping today, 6 hours tramp up steep hills and down steep hills, in mud and water shoe-deep, and in a steady pouring rain which never moderated a moment. I was as chipper and fresh as a lark all the way and arrived without the slightest sense of fatigue. But we were soaked and my shoes full of water, so we ate at once, stripped and went to bed for 2 ½ hours while our traps were thoroughly dried, and our boots greased in addition. Then we put our clothes on hot and went to table d'hote.

Made some nice English friends and shall see them at Zermatt tomorrow.

Gathered a small bouquet of new flowers, but they got spoiled. I sent you a safety-match box full of flowers last night from Leukerbad.

I have just telegraphed you to wire the family news to me at Riffel tomorrow. I do hope you are all well and having as jolly a time as we are, for I love you, sweetheart, and also, in a measure, the Bays [his small daughter's word for 'babies']. Give my love to Clara Spaulding and also to the cubs.

SAML.

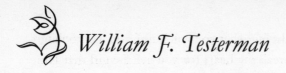

William F. Testerman

All that is known of William F. Testerman is that he was a first lieutenant in Company C of the 8th Tennessee Cavalry during the American Civil War.

To Miss Jane Davis
Gallotin, Tenn, 25 July 1864

Dear Miss,

I again take the opportunity of Droping you a few lines in answer to your kind letters which I received a few days ago one bearing date June '23' the other June the 24 it was a pleasure to me to have the honor to receive a letter from as charming a young girl as the one whos name was asscirbed at the bottom of each of them I was glad to hear that you was well but I was more glad to hear you express your mind as fully as what you did this note leaves me well and I truly hope that this will find you in good health I can't say anthing to you by letter more than what you have heard from my letters before + Jane I hope the time will soon come when I can get to see you again I can write many things to you but if I could see you I could tell you more in one minute than I can rite in aweek The letters that you wrote to me has proved verry satisfactory to meif you will stand up to what you told me in your letters I will be satisfied which I have no reasons to Doubt but what you will but if you was to fail it would almost break my heart for you are the girl that Iam Depending upon and if it was not for you I would not be riting by mycandle to night as you wrote to me that many miles seperated us in person if my heart was like yours we would be united in heart you kneed not to Dout Though we are fare apart at present my heart is with you everymoment for I often think of you when you are alseep when Travailing the lonesom roads in middle Tenn The thought of your sweet smiles is all the company I have I trust that you are cinsere in what you have wrote to me Your sparkling blue eys and rosey red cheeks has gaind my whole efections I hope for the time to come when we shall meet again then if you are in the notion that I am we can pass off the time in pleasure My time has come for sleep and I must soon close I want you to rite to me as soon as you can for I will be glad to hear from you any time Direct your letters as before and dont forget your best friends so I will end my few lines but mylove to you has no Endremember me as ever your love and friend. Excusebad riting.

William F. Testerman

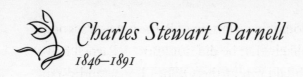

Charles Stewart Parnell
1846–1891

Charles Stewart Parnell, 'the uncrowned king of Ireland', was an unlikely Irish nationalist. He was from landed Protestant gentry, his enthusiasms were hunting and cricket, and having been educated at Cambridge he had the manner and accent of an upper-class Englishman. He was initially a dreadfully shy and nervous public speaker; he was also very superstitious and had a deep aversion to the colour green – something of a problem given his line of work.

Parnell took his seat as a Home Rule MP in 1875. In 1880, at Westminster, he met Mrs Katharine O'Shea, the wife of a fellow Home Rule MP, and the two became lovers almost immediately.

Parnell was imprisoned in Kilmainham Gaol between October 1881 and May 1882, and the letter below dates from that time. Katharine was pregnant with his child, a daughter who was born that February but did not survive.

Katharine's husband, William O'Shea, turned a blind eye to his wife's adultery for ten years, possibly because she was set to inherit a large legacy from an aunt, and would be disinherited if there was a scandal. It seems unlikely that he did not know – Parnell had a cricket pitch laid out at the O'Shea house and established a study there, which must have given O'Shea some idea of what was going on. When the aunt died in 1890, however, he decided the situation was, after all, intolerable and filed for divorce, which was when the public scandal began. The case was a perfect storm of class, money, morality, sex and politics. Katharine was vilified as 'Kitty O'Shea' – 'Kitty' being slang for 'prostitute' – and the divorce ended Parnell's political career. The pair removed to Brighton, where they were married in June 1891; Parnell, whose constitution had always been fragile, died with his wife at his side less than four months later, at the age of forty-five.

To Katharine O'Shea,
Kilmainham, 14 October 1881

My Own Dearest Wifie,
I have found a means of communicating with you, and of your communicating in return.

Please put your letters into enclosed envelope, first putting them in an inner envelope, on the joining of which you can write your initials with a similar pencil to mine, and they will reach me all right. I am very comfortable here, and have a beautiful room facing the sun – the best in the prison. There are three or four of the best of the men in adjoining rooms with whom I can associate all day long, so that time does not hang heavy nor do I feel lonely. My only fear is about my darling Queenie. I have been racked with torture all today, last night, and yesterday, lest the shock may have hurt you or our child. Oh, darling, write or wire me as soon as you get this that you are well and will try not to be unhappy until you see your husband again. You may wire me here.

I have your beautiful face with me here; it is such a comfort. I kiss it every morning.

Your King

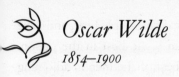

Oscar Wilde
1854–1900

Oscar Wilde was a playwright, novelist, essayist, critic, poet and wit. The effete poses of his youth and his dandyish appearance can still serve to mask his serious intellect: he studied at Trinity College, Dublin and Magdalen, Oxford, graduating with a double first in classics – not the achievement of someone who spent his time at university lolling about dispensing barbed witticisms. He believed in beauty – in dress and furnishings, certainly, but also in art and human relations. He is often written about as though his Irish nationality were basically an accident and to all intents and purposes he was an Englishman, but his sense of himself as Irish was strong, and politically, he was a supporter of Parnell.

Wilde married Constance Mary Lloyd, a Dublin Protestant, in 1884; she gave birth to two sons in quick succession. In 1891, Wilde met Lord Alfred Douglas, son of the Marquess of Queensberry. His subsequent love affair with 'Bosie' effectively ruined his life. In 1895, Douglas's father, famously aggressive, infuriated by his son's relationship with Wilde, left a card at Wilde's club inscribed 'To Oscar Wilde –

posing as Somdomite [sic]'. Wilde made the unwise decision to sue for libel. The case went to court but was abandoned. The vindictive Marquess pursued Wilde through the office of the public prosecutor, which resulted in his standing trial on various counts of gross indecency. He was found guilty and sentenced to two years' hard labour; he served his sentence at Pentonville and then at Reading.

Wilde left prison physically and psychologically destroyed. Popular belief has it that he was abandoned by Douglas, but in fact, Lord Alfred wrote letters to the newspapers protesting the sentence, and petitioned the Queen for clemency. On his release, Wilde drifted from place to place (Constance had not divorced him, but had moved away, and changed her and the childrens' surname), frequently meeting up with Douglas. He died in a Paris hotel room in 1900, declaring a few days beforehand, 'My wallpaper and I are fighting a duel to the death. One or other of us has to go.'

To Lord Alfred Douglas, March 1893
Sent from the Savoy Hotel, London

Dearest of all Boys,
Your letter was delightful, red and yellow wine to me; but I

am sad and out of sorts. Bosie, you must not make scenes with me. They kill me, they wreck the loveliness of life. I cannot see you, so Greek and gracious, distorted with passion. I cannot listen to your curved lips saying hideous things to me. I would sooner be blackmailed by every renter in London than have you bitter, unjust, hating. I must see you soon. You are the divine thing I want, the thing of grace and beauty; but I don't know how to do it. Shall I come to Salisbury? My bill here is £49 for a week. I have also got a new sitting-room over the Thames. Why are you not here, my dear, my wonderful boy? I fear I must leave, no money, no credit, and a heart of lead.

Your own Oscar

To Lord Alfred Douglas
Sent from Courtfield Gardens, 20 May 1895

My child,
Today it was asked to have the verdicts rendered separately. Taylor is probably being judged at this moment, so that I have been able to come back here. My sweet rose, my delicate flower, my lily of lilies, it is perhaps in prison that I am going to test the power of love. I am going to see if I cannot make the bitter warders sweet by the intensity of the love I bear you. I have had moments when I thought it would be wiser to separate. Ah! moments of weakness and madness! Now I see that that would have mutilated my life, ruined my art, broken the musical chords which make

a perfect soul. Even covered with mud I shall praise you, from the deepest abysses I shall cry to you. In my solitude you will be with me. I am determined not to revolt but to accept every outrage through devotion to love, to let my body be dishonoured so long as my soul may always keep the image of you. From your silken hair to your delicate feet you are perfection to me. Pleasure hides love from us, but pain reveals it in its essence. O dearest of created things, if someone wounded by silence and solitude comes to you, dishonoured, a laughing-stock, Oh! you can close his wounds by touching them and restore his soul which unhappiness had for a moment smothered. Nothing will be difficult for you then, and remember, it is that hope which makes me live, and that hope alone. What wisdom is to the philosopher, what God is to his saint, you are to me. To keep you in my soul, such is the goal of this pain which men call life. O my love, you whom I cherish above all things, white narcissus in an unmown field, think of the burden which falls to you, a burden which love alone can make light. But be not saddened by that, rather be happy to have filled with an immortal love the soul of a man who now weeps in hell, and yet carries heaven in his heart. I love you, I love you, my heart is a rose which your love has brought to bloom, my life is a desert fanned by the delicious breeze of your breath, and whose cool spring are your eyes; the imprint of your little feet makes valleys of shade for me, the odour of your hair is like myrrh, and wherever you go you exhale the perfumes of the cassia tree.

Love me always, love me always. You have been the supreme, the perfect love of my life; there can be no other.

I decided that it was nobler and more beautiful to stay. We could not have been together. I did not want to be called a coward or a deserter. A false name, a disguise, a hunted life, all that is not for me, to whom you have been revealed on that high hill where beautiful things are transfigured.

O sweetest of all boys, most loved of all loves, my soul clings to your soul, my life is your life, and in all the world of pain and pleasure you are my ideal of admiration and joy.

Oscar

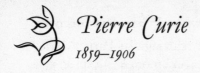

Pierre Curie
1859–1906

When Pierre Curie met Marie Sklodovska at the Sorbonne in 1894, she was a penniless student from Poland. Marie was twenty-four when she arrived in Paris. Despite having no money, and having to pursue her studies in a language in which she was far from fluent, Marie took her mathematics degree at the head of her class in 1893, and her physics degree second in her class a year later.

Pierre had already established himself as a brilliant physicist when the two of them met; what they shared was a fierce idealism, an almost terrifying single-mindedness and a complete lack of interest in plaudits or status. The letter here was written about a year before they married; Marie had been intending to return to Poland, and Pierre is clearly trying, in a very shy and endearing way, to persuade her that they should be together.

The Curies' relationship was quite extraordinarily productive. Working together in a tiny shed, they discovered two new elements, radium and polonium (the latter named for Marie's country of birth), and were awarded half the Nobel Prize in Physics in 1903.

Tragedy struck in 1906, when Pierre was run over and killed by a horse-drawn carriage in Paris. Marie, left with two young daughters, was grief-stricken, but her strength of purpose saw her through, and in 1908, she was appointed the first ever female professor at the Sorbonne; in 1911 she was awarded the Nobel Prize in Chemistry.

Both Marie and Pierre displayed signs of radiation sickness during their lifetime – Pierre liked to carry a sample of radium in his waistcoat pocket to show people, and Marie kept radium salt by her bed that shone in the darkness. Marie died of leukaemia in 1934 and was the first woman to be buried in the Pantheon in Paris. The papers the Curies left behind give off significant radiation, and scholars today wishing to look at their notebooks in the Bibliothèque Nationale must first sign a waiver.

To Marie Sklodovska, 10 August 1894

Nothing could have given me greater pleasure than to get news of you. The prospect of remaining two months without hearing about you had been extremely disagreeable to me: that is to say, your little note was more than welcome.

I hope you are laying up a stock of good air and that you

will come back to us in October. As for me, I think I shall not go anywhere; I shall stay in the country, where I spend the whole day in front of my open window or in the garden.

We have promised each other – haven't we? – to be at least great friends. If you will only not change your mind! For there are no promises that are binding; such things cannot be ordered at will. It would be a fine thing, just the same, in which I hardly dare believe, to pass our lives near each other, hypnotized by our dreams: *your* patriotic dreams, *our* humanitarian dream, and *our* scientific dream.

Of all those dreams the last is, I believe, the only legitimate one. I mean by that we are powerless to change the social order and, even if we were not, we should not know what to do; in taking action, no matter in what direction, we should never be sure of not doing more harm than good, by retarding some inevitable evolution. From the scientific point of view, on the contrary, we may hope to do something; the ground is solider here, and any discovery that we may make, however small, will remain acquired knowledge.

See how it works out: it is agreed that we shall be great friends, but if you leave France in a year it would be an altogether too Platonic friendship, that of two creatures who would never see each other again. Wouldn't it be better for you to stay with me? I know that this question angers you, and that you don't want to speak of it again – and then, too, I feel so thoroughly unworthy of you from every point of view.

I thought of asking your permission to meet you *by chance* in Freibourg. But you are staying there, unless I am mistaken, only one day, and on that day you will of course belong to our friends the Kovalskis.

Believe me your very devoted

Pierre Curie

I should be happy if you would write to me and give me the assurance that you intend to come back in October. If you write direct to Sceaux the letters would get to me quicker: Pierre Curie, 13 rue des Sablons, Sceaux (Seine).

G. K. Chesterton
1874–1936

Gilbert Keith Chesterton is not widely read today, and
is probably best known for his 'Father Brown' detec-
tive stories, but during his lifetime he was a bestselling
novelist, a noted wit and a literary celebrity. He had a
formidable intellect but a wayward mind; he attended
art school and flirted with the idea of a political
career, but it was only when he began writing journalism for the thriving magazine and newspaper market
of 1890s London that he found his place in the world.

Chesterton as a boy and young man had no interest
in religion, but as he reached his twenties he was
increasingly attracted to Christianity. He met Frances
Blogg, the daughter of a diamond merchant of
French descent, in 1896, and her devout Anglo-
Catholicism informed his own religious beliefs. His
letter to her below is a model of charm, self-depreca-
tion, wit and affection. They were married in 1901.

It was in the years leading up to the Great War
that Chesterton's fame was at its height. He certainly
cut an arresting figure; vast (six foot four) and vastly
overweight, he habitually wore a cloak and a broad-
brimmed hat, and was a fixture in the public houses

around Fleet Street. (A famous anecdote has him telling his friend George Bernard Shaw, 'To look at you, anyone would think there was a famine in England,' to which Shaw replied, 'To look at you, anyone would think you caused it.')

In 1909, Frances decided that he needed to be removed from London and its temptations, and they moved to Beaconsfield in Buckinghamshire. Their marriage was happy, although their not having children was a source of sadness to both.

Chesterton's post-war writing was increasingly religious and mystical, and he finally converted to Catholicism in 1922. His work was disfigured by anti-Semitism, and while his admirers have made the case that it was variously 1) not that extreme and 2) part and parcel of the time in which he lived, the accusation cannot be dismissed. He died in 1936 at home in Beaconsfield; Frances survived him.

To Frances Blogg (189–?)

. . . I am looking over the sea and endeavouring to reckon up the estate I have to offer you. As far as I can make out my equipment for starting on a journey to fairyland consists of the following items.

1st. A Straw Hat. The oldest part of this admirable relic shows traces of pure Norman work. The vandalism of Cromwell's soldiers has left us little of the original hat-band.

2nd. A Walking Stick, very knobby and heavy: admirably fitted to break the head of any denizen of Suffolk who denies that you are the noblest of ladies, but of no other manifest use.

3rd. A copy of Walt Whitman's poems, once nearly given to Salter, but quite forgotten. It has his name in it still with an affectionate inscription from his sincere friend Gilbert Chesterton. I wonder if he will ever have it.

4th. A number of letters from a young lady, containing everything good and generous and loyal and holy and wise that isn't in Walt Whitman's poems.

5th. An unwieldy sort of a pocket knife, the blades mostly having an edge of a more varied and picturesque outline than is provided by the prosaic cutler. The chief element however is a thing 'to take the stones out of a horse's hoof'. What a beautiful sensation of security it gives one to reflect that if one should ever have money enough to buy a horse and should happen to have a stone in his hoof — that one is ready; one stands prepared, with a defiant smile!

6th. Passing from the last miracle of practical foresight, we come to a box of matches. Every now and then I strike one of these, because fire is beautiful and burns your fingers. Some people think this a waste of matches: the same people who object to the building of Cathedrals.

7th. About three pounds in gold and silver, the remains

of one of Mr Unwin's bursts of affection: those explosions of spontaneous love for myself, which, such is the perfect order and harmony of his mind, occur at startlingly exact intervals of time.

8th. A book of Children's Rhymes, in manuscript, called 'Weather Book' about ? finished, and destined for Mr Nutt. I have been working at it fairly steadily, which I think jolly creditable under the circumstances. One can't put anything interesting in it. They'll understand those things when they grow up.

9th. A tennis racket – nay, start not. It is a part of the new regime, and the only new and neat-looking thing in the Museum. We'll soon mellow it – like the straw hat. My brother and I are teaching each other lawn tennis.

10th. A soul, hitherto idle and omnivorous but now happy enough to be ashamed of itself.

11th. A body, equally idle and quite equally omnivorous, absorbing tea, coffee, claret, sea-water and oxygen to its own perfect satisfaction. It is happiest swimming, I think, the sea being a convenient size.

12th. A Heart – mislaid somewhere. And that is about all the property of which an inventory can be made at present. After all, my tastes are stoically simple. A straw hat, a stick, a box of matches and some of his own poetry. What more does man require?

Letters from the Great War

Captain Alfred Bland

Written while serving in France with the 22nd Battalion of the Manchester Regiment, to his wife Violet. Bland was killed on 1 July 1916, the first day of the Battle of the Somme.

To Violet

My only and eternal blessedness,
I wonder whether you resent my cheerfulness ever! Do you, dear? Because you might, you know. I ought, by the rules of love, to spend my days and nights in an eternity of sighs and sorrow for our enforced parting. And by all the rules of war, I ought to be enduring cold and hardship, hunger and fatigue, bitterness of soul and dismay of heart.

Alas! What shall I say in my defence? Because not even Merriman can depress me, and as for the CO, I am simply impertinent to him, while the dull routine of being behind the line fills me with an inexhaustible supply of cheerful patience. What shall we say about it? Would it rejoice you if I confessed to being utterly miserable every now and then? If I told you how I loathed war and hated every minute that prolonged it? If I admitted that I yearn hourly for my return, my final return away from it all? If I said that

I hated my brother officers and was sick of the sight of the Company? If I described the filthy squalor of the village streets, the sickening repetition of low clouds and sulky drizzle and heavy rain, and the dreary monotony of ration beef and ration bread? Would you be glad or sorry?

Oh, I know how sympathetic and sad you would feel, and I know you would not be glad at all. Would you? And if you were glad, you would be all wrong; because, even if those things were true, it wouldn't bring us together again, it wouldn't make me love you more, it wouldn't sweeten those embraces we are deprived of for the moment, it wouldn't strengthen our divine oneness one scrap. Would it?

No, my darling, thank the heavens daily that in all circumstances you will be right in picturing your boy out here simply brimming over with gaiety irrepressible. I am becoming a byword. Cushion says, 'I like you, Bill Bland.' Why? Because I am always laughing with everybody and everything, greeting the seen and the unseen with a cheer. And it isn't a pose. It's the solemn truth.

So let us go back again to those imaginary admissions above. I am never utterly miserable, not even when I yearn most for the touch of your lips and a sight of my boys. Why? Because I am in France, where the war is, and I know I ought to be here. And I don't loathe war, I love ninety-five per cent of it, and hate the thought of it being ended too soon. And I don't yearn hourly for my final return, although I am very pleasantly excited at the possibility of nine days' leave in March, which indeed we haven't earned by any means so far.

And I don't loathe my brother officers but love them more than I dreamed possible, and as for my Company, why bless it! And the mud is such friendly mud, somehow, so yielding and considerate – and I don't have to clean my own boots. And I have lost the habit of regarding the weather, for if it rains, we get wet, and if it doesn't, we don't, and if the sun shines, how nice! And as for our food, well, I've given you an idea of that before, and I have nothing to add to the statements made in this House on November 30 and December 6 last or any other time.

No, dear, whether you like it or not, I am fundamentally happy and on the surface childishly gay. And there's an end on't.

Post just going.

Good night, darling.

Ever your

Alfred

Regimental Sergeant-Major James Milne

James 'Jim' Milne was a company sergeant-major who served with the 4th Battalion, Gordon Highlanders. The following is a farewell letter to his wife Meg, in the event of his being killed in battle.

Milne came through the war, and returned home to Scotland.

My own beloved wife,

I do not know how to start this letter. The circumstances
are different from any under which I ever wrote before.
I am not to post it but will leave it in my pocket, and if
anything happens to me, someone will perhaps post it.
We are going over the top this forenoon and only God
in Heaven knows who will come out of it alive. I am going
into it now, Dearest, sure that I am in His hands and that
whatever happens, I look to Him, in this world and the
world to come.

If I am called, my regret is that I leave you and my
Bairns, but I leave you all to His great mercy and goodness,
knowing that He will look over you all and watch you. I
trust in Him to bring me through, but should He decree
otherwise then though we do not know His reasons, we
know it must be best. I go to Him with your dear face the
last vision on earth I shall see and your name upon my lips.
You, the best of Women. You will look after my Darling
Bairns for me and tell them how their Daddy died.

Oh! How I love you all, and as I sit here waiting I wonder what you are doing at home. I must not do that. It is
hard enough sitting waiting. We may move at any minute.
When this reaches you, for me there will be no more war –
only eternal peace and waiting for you.

You must be brave, my Darling, for my sake, for I leave
you the Bairns. It is a legacy of struggle for you, but God

will look after you and we shall meet again when there will be no more parting. I am to write no more, Sweetheart. I know you will read my old letters and keep them for my sake, and that you will love me or my memory till we meet again.

May God in his Mercy look over you and bless you all till that day we shall met again in His own Good time. May He in that same Mercy preserve me today.

GoodBye Meg,
Eternal love from
Yours for Ever and Ever,
Jim

Second Lieutenant John Lindsay Rapoport

John Rapoport, aged twenty-four, became engaged during the spring of 1918; the letter below is to his fiancée. At the beginning of June, he was posted missing during the third battle of the Aisne. His body was never recovered.

6 May 1918

The mail has just come in and I've got fourteen letters! Among them, my darling, were five from you. So you can imagine what I feel like. I got the very first one of all tonight, the one you sent to me at Havre. They've been awfully slack in forwarding it.

Darling, you were just splendid when you saw me off at Waterloo. You just typified the women of England by your attitude, everything for us men, and you have your dark times to yourselves so as not to depress us . . .

You mean so much to me, you have no idea how much. Life without you would be absolutely empty. I wonder however I got on before. As a matter of fact, I am full of love and for the last two or three years I've had a longing to pour it out on someone, and I've always lived in the hope of doing so – that kept me going. Now I've got someone on whom I can and have lavished all my love.

My darling, I love and adore you from the bottom of my heart. You wait till I come home – you will get some kisses then, and I shall hold you tight – you know how, my darling, don't you?

I am so glad we are both alike on the question of friends. Of course I want you to carry on with your men friends just as if I didn't exist. One thing I am [as] sure of as that I exist: that is that I have all your heart and all your love. So I just want you to enjoy yourself – I love you so much. Have a topping time on the river and at shows, etc, with your friends, won't you?

I asked WW to write to me still, though we were engaged – just as friends. I feel very sorry for your friends. Just impress on them that you can be chums just as before. I know it isn't quite the same, but I should like it, because I know what a help you'd be to any man. Just thank your friends for their good wishes, will you?

Oh, the more I think of it, the more I realize how lucky I am in having you for my *own* darling wife-to-be. Oh, hasn't God been good to me – far more than I deserve.

*Love Letters
of Great Women*

Introduction

When *Love Letters of Great Men*, the first half of this collection, was published, it gave rise to a small discussion about whether or not people write love letters any more. The consensus seemed to be that today's instant communication has supplanted words on paper, and it was viewed as even more improbable that a *man* would nowadays put himself out to such an extent as to write a letter (and then post it). But it seemed that what people (and it has to be said mainly women) were lamenting was not the usurping of the love letter by text messaging or email, but rather the passing of an age when men actually talked about their feelings rather than grunting from the sofa. There was an appetite for reading the romantic (and not so romantic) outpourings of various men from history, perhaps not because of who those men were, but because such outpourings are thin on the ground today – in any form.

Those letters, as I wrote at the time, varied enormously in style, sentiment and (sad to say) sincerity – it did sometimes seem as though some Great Men wrote with an eye to posterity, or believed that a love letter was just another vehicle for demonstrating their creative brilliance. Compiling this volume was a very different reading experience. For the Great Men of history, the matter of who they loved and who they might marry was but one aspect of their lives; their Greatness rested on their achievements in other spheres: scientific discovery, exploration, conquest, political triumph, artistic endeavour. These avenues were not open to most women until shockingly recently, and it is a sad fact that the Greatness of many of the women in this collection rests either on who they married or to whom they gave birth; their connection with their illustrious spouses or off-spring was the only reason their letters were preserved at all. For many of the women here, marriage would determine their entire destiny. I cannot (and of course would not) claim that women are more often sincere than men, or less capable of dissimulation and posturing; the point is that affairs of the heart could irrevocably alter the course of a woman's life in a way they did not a man's. It is hard to imagine any of the Great Men writing, as Lady Mary Wortley Montagu did to her beloved before eloping with him against her father's wishes in 1712, 'I tremble for what we are doing. Are you sure you will love me for ever? Shall we never repent? I fear, and I hope.' For a woman, the consequences of making the wrong decision, of playing the wrong hand, could be nothing short of disastrous.

There are women here, of course, who did flout convention, disobeyed their families and fought to take control of their lives. But in the main these women were exceptionally brilliant, independently wealthy, or both. Which is to take nothing away from their achievements; it is simply worth noting that the bar to success for women was set almost impossibly high. And of course there are other women in the collection who were actively encouraged and helped by the wonderful men they married – Abigail Adams and Isabella Beeton, for instance, seem to have had husbands who, hearteningly, wanted them to succeed at all they did.

There are sad stories here – not only of the love affairs that ended badly, but also of the danger and heartbreak women endured in so many aspects of their lives, from their powerlessness and lack of education and economic independence to the deadly hazards presented by childbirth and the likelihood of those children dying very young. Antibiotics and the vote changed everything – at least in the more economically developed world (it is worth noting the terrible statistic from the UN that of the 536,000 maternal deaths each year, 99 per cent now occur in less economically developed countries). This doesn't feel like a 'You've come a long way, baby' moment, but it is sometimes good to remember how much progress women have made since Mary Wollstonecraft wrote her *Vindication of the Rights of Women* in 1790.

What shines through this collection for me is the resilience of these women in the face of what seem insuperable difficulties: their bravery, their stoicism, their wit, their charm and their generosity. The love written here comes in many forms – tolerant, deluded, ambiguous, ambitious, selfish, erotic, chaste and mad – but love it is, and a legacy to cherish.

Ursula Doyle, London, 2010

'I used to look at all these daft girls, marrying the first
fellow they thought they could live with. And I suppose
I was waiting for the fellow I couldn't live without.'

Nora Doyle, 1917–2007

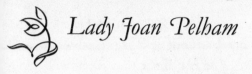

Lady Joan Pelham

This 1399 letter from Lady Pelham to her husband, Sir John, was written from their home at Pevensey Castle in East Sussex. Sir John Pelham was away, helping Henry Bolingbroke to rally troops for what became a successful attempt to wrest the throne from Richard II. Pevensey was besieged by her husband's enemies; Lady Pelham, without wishing to make a fuss, is enquiring whether he might be returning soon.

To Sir John Pelham, (15 July?) 1399

My dear Lord,

I recommend me to your high lordship, with heart and body and all my poor might. And with all this I thank you as my dear Lord, dearest and best beloved of all earth lords. I say for me, and thank you, my dear Lord, with all this that I said before for your comfortable letter that you sent me from Pontefract, that came to me on Mary Magdalen's day; for by my troth I was never so glad as when I heard by your letter ye were strong enough with the Grace of God to keep you from the malice of your enemies. And, dear Lord, if it like to your high Lordship that as soon as ye might that I might hear of your gracious speed, which God Almighty continue and increase. And, my dear Lord, if it like you to know *my* fare, I am here laid by in a manner of a siege with the County of Sussex, Surrey and a great parcel of Kent, so that I may not go out nor no victuals get me, but with much hazard. Wherefore, my dear, if it like you by the advice of your wise counsel for to set remedy to the salvation of your castle and withstand the malice of the shires aforesaid. And also that ye be fully informed of the great malice-workers in these shires which have so despitefully wrought to you, and to your castle, to your men, and to your tenants; for this country have they wasted for a great while.

Farewell, my dear Lord! the Holy Trinity keep you from your enemies, and soon send me good tidings of you. Written at Pevensey, in the castle, on St Jacob's day last past, by your own poor J. Pelham. To my true Lord.

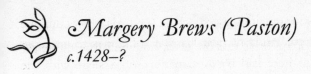

Margery Brews (Paston)
c.1428–?

The Pastons were a prominent Norfolk family of the late medieval period who left behind a treasure trove of letters covering four generations, which paint a vivid picture of life at the time. The letters below, from Margery Brews to John Paston, written in 1476, are sometimes described as the oldest love letters in the English language but in fact they are more businesslike than they might at first appear. Their primary topic is the ongoing negotiations over the size of Margery's dowry, which the Paston family considered too small. Margery and John did eventually marry in 1477.

To John Paston
Sent from Topcroft, February 1476

Unto my right well-beloved Valentine, John Paston, Esq., be this Bill delivered, &c.

Right reverend and worshipful, and my right well-beloved Valentine, I recommend me unto you, full heartily desiring to hear of your welfare, which I beseech Almighty God long for to preserve unto his pleasure and your heart's desire.

And if it please you to hear of my welfare, I am not in good heele of body nor of heart, nor shall I be till I hear from you.

For there wottys [knows] no creature what pain that I endure,
And for to be dead, I dare it not dyscur

And my lady my mother hath laboured the matter to my father full diligently, but she can no more get than ye know of, for the which God knoweth I am full sorry. But if that ye love me, as I trust verily that ye do, ye will not leave me therefore; for if that ye had not half the livelihood that ye have, for to do the greatest labour that any woman alive might, I would not forsake you.

And if ye command me to keep me true wherever I go,
I wis I will de all my might you to love, and never no mo.
And if my friends say that I do amiss,
They shall not me let so for to do,
Mine heart me bids evermore to love you
Truly over all earthly thing,
And if they be never so wrath,
I trust it shall be better in time coming.

No more to you at this time, but the Holy Trinity have you in keeping; and I beseech you that this bill be not seen of none earthly creature save only yourself, &c.

And this letter was endited at Topcroft, with fully heavy heart, &c.

By your own
Margery Brews

To John Paston

I thank you with all my heart for the letter you sent me . . . from which I know for certain that you intend to come . . . shortly, with no other errand or business except to bring to a conclusion the business between my father and you. I would be the happiest one alive if only the business might come to fruition . . . And if you come and the business comes to nothing, then I will be even sorrier and full of sadness.

As for myself, I have done and endured in the business as much as I know how or am able to, God knows. And I want you to understand clearly that my father refuses to part with any more money than one hundred [pounds] and fifty marks in this business, which is far from fulfilling your wishes.

For which reason, if you could be content with that amount and my poor person, I would be the happiest maid on earth. And if you do not consider yourself satisfied with that, or believe that you could get more money, as I have understood from you before, good, faithful and loving Valentine, do not take the trouble to visit anymore on this business. Rather let it be finished and never spoken of again, on condition that I may be your faithful friend and petitioner for the duration of my life.

No more to you now, but may Almighty Jesus preserve you, in both body and soul.

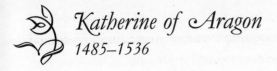

Katherine of Aragon
1485–1536

Katherine of Aragon was born at the palace at Alcalá de Henares, north-east of Madrid, on 16 December 1485, the daughter of Ferdinand of Aragon and Isabella of Castile. Isabella was determined that her daughters should have a good education based on Catholic principles. Katherine's knowledge of Latin, European languages and classical literature was widely admired, and she was extremely devout.

When the princess was only two, Henry VII of England proposed a match between Katherine and his eldest son, Arthur, Prince of Wales, who was a year younger than the prospective bride. After negotiations lasting more than ten years, the princess arrived in Plymouth in October 1501, and the marriage between Katherine of Aragon and Arthur, Prince of Wales, was solemnized in St Paul's on 14 November.

By the following April, at the age of fifteen, Arthur was dead. The Spanish immediately expressed an interest in Katherine marrying Henry, the new Prince of Wales. Henry VII was at first amenable, but negotiations dragged on in England, in Spain and in Rome (a dispensation was needed from the Pope, because Henry was Katherine's former brother-in-law) for six years. Katherine remained in London as dowager Princess of Wales; she was homesick and short of money, frequently complaining to her father about the tight-fisted behaviour of Henry VII. By March 1509, she was begging to be allowed to return to Spain and enter a convent. Henry and Katherine were finally married in June 1509, just weeks after Henry succeeded to the throne.

The length of the marriage – more than twenty years – is often eclipsed by what followed; Henry's five subsequent marriages took place over ten tumultuous years from 1533. It also appears that the pair were content for much of their married life, although Katherine's many miscarriages and stillbirths must have taken their toll – her only surviving child was Princess Mary, born in 1516. Katherine exists in popular myth as a dumpy, depressed religious maniac, with her rosary beads, broken English and unglamorous gynaecological problems, but the evidence suggests that Henry respected his wife to the extent that she took charge of affairs of state in his absence – notwithstanding her unshakeable belief that a wife's Christian duty was to obey her husband in all things. The first letter below was written while Henry was off fighting the French; Katherine had successfully repelled a Scottish invasion led by James IV, and the king himself had been left dead in the field. She gleefully writes of sending Henry the dead monarch's coat, implying that she would rather have liked to send his body, but her squeamish English courtiers would not allow it.

The rupture between Henry and Katherine was a more complicated business than one might be led to believe from its numerous portrayals in fiction, where it comes about through Henry's boredom with his ageing wife and his enslavement by the bewitching Anne Boleyn. If these were factors, there were several others, including the dwindling importance of the alliance with Spain, and Henry's obsession with producing a male heir. There is no doubt, however, that his treatment of Katherine was horrible. He put her through a humiliating trial concerning the consummation of her marriage to his brother, and after the annulment kept her apart from her beloved daughter, who he had proclaimed illegitimate.

After Anne Boleyn was installed as queen, Katherine was sent to the provinces, first to Huntingdon and then to Cambridgeshire. She refused to recognize Anne's title, refused to accept her own of princess dowager, and refused to sign an oath recognizing

Anne's children as the legitimate successors to Henry. She died in 1536, steadfastly proclaiming that her marriage to Henry was valid, that she was queen, and that she continued to love her husband. Her final letter to him, the second below, is heartbreaking: 'Lastly, do I vow, that mine eyes desire you above all things.' Henry and Anne marked her death by dressing in yellow and parading their daughter, the baby Princess Elizabeth, around the court.

To Henry VIII, 16 September 1513

Sir, My Lord Howard hath sent me a letter open to your Grace, within one of mine, by the which you shall see at length the great Victory that our Lord hath sent your subjects in your absence; and for this cause there is no need herein to trouble your Grace with long writing, but, to my thinking, this battle hath been to your Grace and all your realm the greatest honor that could be, and more than you should win all the crown of France; thanked be God of it, and I am sure your Grace forgetteth not to do this, which shall be cause to send you many more such great victories, as I trust he shall do. My husband, for hastiness, with Rougecross I could not send your Grace the piece of the King of Scots coat which John Glynn now brings. In this your Grace shall see how I keep my promise, sending you for your banners a king's coat. I thought to send himself unto you, but our Englishmens' hearts would not suffer it. It should have been better for him to have been in peace than have this reward. All that God sends is for the best.

My Lord of Surrey, my Henry, would fain know your pleasure in the burying of the King o Scots' body, for he has written to me so. With the next messenger your Grace's pleasure may be herein known. And with this I make an end, praying God to send you home shortly, for without this no joy here can be accomplished; and for the same I pray, and now go to Our Lady of Walsingham that I promised so long ago to see. At Woburn the 16th of September.

I send your Grace herein a bill found in a Scotsman's purse of such things as the French King sent to the said King of Scots to make war against you, beseeching you to send Mathew hither as soon as this messenger comes to bring me tidings from your Grace.

Your humble wife and true servant, Katherine.

To Henry VIII, 1535

My Lord and Dear Husband,
I commend me unto you. The hour of my death draweth fast on, and my case being such, the tender love I owe you forceth me, with a few words, to put you in remembrance of the health and safeguard of your soul, which you ought to prefer before all worldly matters, and before the care and tendering of your own body, for the which you have cast

me into many miseries and yourself into many cares.

For my part I do pardon you all, yea, I do wish and devoutly pray God that He will also pardon you.

For the rest I commend unto you Mary, our daughter, beseeching you to be a good father unto her, as I heretofore desired. I entreat you also, on behalf of my maids, to give them marriage-portions, which is not much, they being but three. For all my other servants, I solicit a year's pay more than their due, lest they should be unprovided for.

Lastly, do I vow, that mine eyes desire you above all things.

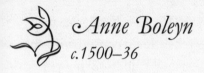

Anne Boleyn
c.1500–36

Anne Boleyn was the daughter of Thomas Boleyn, Earl of Ormond, and Elizabeth Howard, the daughter of Thomas Howard, Duke of Norfolk. Thomas Boleyn was enormously ambitious for his three children, of whom Anne was the second, and when at the age of thirteen she was offered a position as a lady-in-waiting at the court of Margaret of Austria in Brussels, he saw it as an unmissable opportunity. Margaret's was among the most prestigious courts of Europe, and would equip Anne for the ultimate prize, a place at the court of Katherine of Aragon. But shortly after her arrival in Brussels, the diplomatic situation changed, and Anne was moved to France, where she entered the service of Claude, the queen. The two became close, and Anne acquired a polish and glamour that was immediately apparent when she returned to the English court in 1521 – accomplished, tasteful, witty and beautifully dressed, she was absolutely unlike her contemporaries.

The next step for Anne was marriage, but several avenues of enquiry came to nothing, possibly because in her father's eyes the suitors on offer were insufficiently grand. And then, in 1526 or thereabouts, Anne caught the eye of Henry VIII. The king was ready for a new mistress, having recently dispensed with the services of Mary, Anne's sister. But it so happened that the vacancy coincided with Henry's growing conviction, in the absence of a male heir, that his marriage to Katherine had never been valid.

The annulment of Henry and Katherine's marriage and his subsequent marriage to Anne played out over the next six years. The political and religious fallout was huge, and led ultimately to Henry's break with Rome and the establishment of the Church of England. The couple were finally married in January 1533, when Anne was just pregnant; Princess Elizabeth was born on 7 September.

It was not a disaster for Anne that her first child was a girl; she was still young. But a miscarriage in August 1534 did not augur well, and she did not conceive again until the autumn of 1535. In January 1536, Katherine died, which came as a relief to Henry and Anne, who knew how much support she and her daughter, Mary, retained in the country at large; this relief was short-lived, as Anne had another miscarriage at the end of the same month. Still, the situation might have been salvageable, had it not been for Anne's falling out with the Lord Chancellor, Thomas Cromwell, previously a key ally, and for important diplomatic negotiations being scuppered by Henry's insistence that powerful European monarchs recognize Anne as his lawful wife.

Anne had to go, and Thomas Cromwell arranged it. A mere divorce would not suffice; Anne and her faction had to be permanently dispatched. So Cromwell cooked up a selection of terrible charges, accusing her not only of incestuous relations with her brother George, but adultery with four other men of her circle. All were arrested and taken to the Tower.

After trials of non-existent legality, George Boleyn and his co-accused were executed on 17 May 1536, and that afternoon the Archbishop of Canterbury declared Anne and Henry's marriage null and void on the grounds of Henry's previous association with Mary Boleyn (which rather begs the question of how an unmarried Anne managed to commit the alleged adultery). On 19 May, Anne was executed on Tower Green by a swordsman brought over from France in order to spare her the axe. It was less than six months since the death of Katherine of Aragon. On 30 May Henry married Jane Seymour, one of Anne's ladies-in-waiting.

The letter below, dated 6 May, exists only as a copy, and so its authenticity has not been established.

To Henry VIII, 6 May 1536

Sir,

Your graces displeasure, and my Imprisonment are things so
Strange unto me, and what to write or what to excuse, I am
altogether ignorant, whereas you send unto me (willing me
to confess a truth and so to obtain your favour) by such
a one, whom you know to be my ancient professed enemy,
I no sooner received this message by him, than I right con-
ceived your meaning; and if as you say confessing a truth
in deed, may procure my safety, I shall with all willingness
and duty perform your Command; but let not your grace
ever imagine that your poor wife, will ever be brought to
acknowledge fault where not so much as a thought thereof
proceeded, and to speak a truth, never prince had wife more
Loyal in all duty, and in all true affection, than you have ever
found in Anne Boleyn, with which name and place I could
willingly have contented myself, if so god and your graces
pleasure had been pleased. Neither did I at any time so far
forget my self in my exaltation, or received queenship, but
that I always looked for such an alteration as now I find, for
the ground of my preferment being on no surer foundation
than your graces fancy, the least alteration, I knew was fit
and sufficient to draw that fancy to some other subject.

You have chosen me from a low estate to be your Queen
and Companion, far beyond my desert or desire, if then you
found me worthy of such honour, good your grace, let not
any light fancy or bad counsel of my enemies, withdraw

your princely favour from me, neither let that stain, that unworthy stain of a disloyal heart towards your grace ever cast so foul a blot on your most dutiful wife and the infant princess your daughter; try me good king, but let me have a lawful trial, and let not my sworn enemies sit as my accusers and judges; yea let me receive an open trial, for my truth shall fear no open shames; then shall you see either my innocency cleared, your suspicion and conscience satisfied, the ignominy and slander of the world stopped, or my guilt openly declared; so that what so ever God or you may determine of me, your grace may be freed from an open censure, and my offence being so lawfully proved, your grace is at liberty, both before God and man, not only to execute worthy punishment on me as an unfaithful wife, but to follow your affection already settled on that party, for whose sake I come now as I am, whose name I could some good while sith have pointed unto your grace, being not ignorant of my suspicion therein.

But if you have already determined of me, and that not only my death but an infamous slander must bring you the enjoying your desired happiness, then I desire of God that he will pardon your greater sin herein, and likewise my enemies, the instruments thereof; and if he will not call you to a straight account for your unprincely and cruel usage of me, at his general Judgement Seat, where both you and my self must shortly appear, and in whose right judgement I doubt not (what so ever the world may think of me), mine innocence shall be openly known, and sufficiently cleared;

my last and only request shall be, that my self may only bear the burthen of your graces displeasure, and that it may not touch the innocent souls of those poor gentlemen whom as I understand are likewise in straight imprisonment for my sake; If ever I have found favour in your sight; if ever the name of Anne Boleyn have been pleasing to your ears let me obtain this last request. And I will so leave to trouble your grace any further, with my earnest prayers to the Trinity to have your grace in his good keeping, and to direct you in all your actions. From my doleful prison in the Tower this 6 of May,

Yr most loyal and faithful wife
A.B.

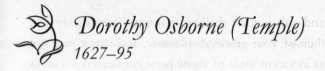

Dorothy Osborne (Temple)
1627–95

Dorothy Osborne was from a family who took the royalist part during England's civil war; her father, Sir Peter Osborne, was the lieutenant-governor of the Channel island of Guernsey. After the outbreak of the civil war, her mother, Lady Dorothy, took her children from their home in Bedfordshire to St Malo in France to be near her husband, who was besieged in Castle Cornet on Guernsey. In 1644, having got herself into debt sending provisions to Sir Peter, Lady Dorothy brought the family back to England, where they resided temporarily in Chelsea at the home of her brother, as Bedfordshire was in the hands of parliamentarian forces. Two of Dorothy's own brothers were killed in the civil war, the second in 1646, the year Sir Peter was forced to retreat from Guernsey and made for St Malo. It was on a voyage out to see her father that Dorothy met Sir William Temple, a young man who was embarking on a continental tour, having left Cambridge without taking his degree.

A lengthy and intermittent courtship ensued. Dorothy's father and her brothers were implacably opposed to the marriage; the Osborne finances had been severely depleted by the war, and they had hoped Dorothy would find a rich husband. In 1648 Sir William departed once more for the Continent, and in 1651, after the lovers managed to meet in London, Dorothy's family returned to Bedfordshire. There she was presented with endless suitable young men, all of whom she rejected. This was when the correspondence between the lovers began in earnest; seventy-seven letters from Dorothy to Sir William survive (she destroyed all but one of Sir William's to her). She had to circumvent the close surveillance of her brother Henry, which meant that her letters had to be smuggled out of the house. It wasn't until 1654, after the death of Dorothy's father, that the two were married, although the opposition of her family was unabated. Dorothy suffered a disfiguring and almost fatal attack of smallpox a month before the wedding.

The couple settled initially in Ireland, where they had eight or nine children (at least six died in infancy, but the records are unclear). In 1665, Sir William was appointed ambassador to the Netherlands, where they remained until 1671. Dorothy and Sir William played a behind-the-scenes role in brokering the marriage of William of Orange and Mary Stuart, the daughter of the Duke of York, who jointly ruled England, Scotland and Ireland from 1689. Dorothy and Mary remained confidantes until Mary's death in 1694.

Dorothy died in 1695 at Moor Park, an estate in Surrey that Sir William had bought for their retirement. She was buried in Westminster Abbey. Her vivacious and witty letters were published in various editions from 1836, which is when her literary reputation was secured.

To Sir William Temple, no date

There are a great many ingredients must go to the making me happy in a husband. First, as my cousin Franklin says, our humours must agree; and to do that he must have that kind of breeding that I have had, and used that kind of company. That is, he must not be so much a country gentleman as to understand nothing but hawks and dogs, and be fonder of either than his wife; nor of the next sort of them whose aim reaches no further than to be Justice of the Peace, and once in his life High Sheriff, who reads no book but Statutes, and studies nothing but how to make a speech interlarded with Latin that may amaze his disagreeing poor neighbours, and fright them rather than persuade them into quietness. He must not be a thing that began the world in a free school, was sent from thence to the university, and is at his furthest when he reaches the Inns of Court, has no acquaintances but those of his form in these places, speaks the French he has picked out of old laws, and admires nothing but the stories he has heard of the revels that were kept there before his time. He must not be a town gallant neither, that lives in a tavern and an ordinary, that cannot imagine how an hour should be spent without company unless it be in sleeping, that makes court to all the women he sees, thinks they believe him, and laughs and is laughed at equally. Nor a travelled Monsieur whose head is all feather inside and outside, than can talk of nothing but dancing and duets, and has courage enough to wear slashes when every one else dies with cold to see him. He must not be a fool of no sort, nor peevish, nor ill-natured, nor proud, nor covetous; and to all this must be added, that he must love me and I him as much as we are capable of loving. Without all this, his fortune, though never so great, would not satisfy me; and with it, a very moderate one would keep me from ever repenting my disposal.

To Sir William Temple, no date

'Twill be pleasinger to you, I am sure, to tell how fond I am of your lock. Well, in earnest now, and setting aside all compliments, I never saw finer hair, nor of a better colour; but cut no more on't, I would not have it spoiled for the world. If you love me, be careful on't. I am combing, and curling, and kissing this lock all day, and dreaming on't all night. The ring, too, is very well, only a little of the biggest. Send me a tortoise one that is a little less than that I sent for a pattern. I would not have the rule so absolutely true without exception that hard hairs be ill-natured, for then I should be so. But I can allow that all soft hairs are good, and so are you, or I am deceived as much as you are if you think I do not love you enough. Tell me, my dearest, am I? You will not be if you think I am

    Yours.

Nell Gwyn
1651?–87

Nell Gwyn is the most celebrated of the (many) mistresses of King Charles II. Almost nothing is known of her early life, although her detractors liked to spread stories that she was variously a herring-seller, a cinder-sweeper and a servant in a brothel. She is popularly believed to have started out in the theatre selling oranges in 1663; Samuel Pepys first saw her acting at Drury Lane in December 1666.

Nell had liaisons with more than one aristocrat before and after she met the king (the letter below is to Lawrence Hyde, later the Earl of Rochester, who was at The Hague on diplomatic business in May and June 1678). She became Charles II's mistress in 1668 or 1669, and bore him a son, Charles, in May 1670. That summer, a grand house was leased for her in Pall Mall ('pel mel', below), acknowledging her position as a (sadly not 'the') royal mistress, and a second son, James, was born there in 1671. Nell lobbied hard for titles for her boys, and in 1676 Charles was given the surname Beauclerk and created Baron Heddington and Earl of Burford.

Nell had influential friends at court, but also enemies who made no secret of their contempt for her low birth, disreputable former occupation, high spirits and lack of social graces. Her chief enemy was another of the king's mistresses, Louise de Kéroualle, Duchess of Portsmouth, who also happened to be French, Catholic and deeply unpopular with the public. One story has Nell's coach surrounded by an angry mob who believed it to belong to the duchess; they were placated only when Nell stuck her head out of the window and cheerfully announced, 'Pray, good people, be silent, I am the Protestant whore.'

Charles II died in 1685; his last words are reputed to have been, 'Let not poor Nelly starve.' His successor, James II, gave her a generous pension, and she died at Pall Mall in 1687. As befits her reputation for charity, she left £100 to the debtors of her parish and £20 a year to release debtors from prison every Christmas day, as well as £50 to poor Catholics, 'for showing my charity to those who differ from me in Religeon'. In his memoirs Gilbert Burnet, the bishop and historian, described her as the 'indiscreetest and wildest creature that ever was in court', which may explain the longevity of her relationship with a king renowned for his love of a good time.

To Lawrence Hyde, c.1678

Pray dear Mr. Hide forgive me for not writeing to you efore now for the reasone is I have bin sick thre months & sinse I have recovered I have had nothing to intertaine you withal nor have nothing now worth writing but that I can holde no longer to let you know I never had ben in any companie without drinking your health for I loue yo with all my soule. The pel mel is now to me a dismal plase since, I have utterly lost Sr Car Scrope [Sir Carr Scrope, a wit of Charles II's circle] never to be recoured agane for he tould me he could not live allwayes at this rate & so begune to be a little uncivil, which I could not sufer from an ugly *baux garscon*. Ms Knights [a singer, and rival for Charles II's affections] Lady mothers dead & she has put up a scutchin [escutcheon] no bigger then my Lady Grins scunchis [escutcheon]. My lord Rochester [John Wilmot, the scandalous poet, who died two years later] is gon in the cuntrei. Mr Savil [Henry Savile, future Vice-Chamberlain] has got a misfortune, but is upon recovery & is to mary an hairres [heiress], who I thinke wont have an ill time ont if he holds up his thumb. My lord of Dorset [a former protector of Nell's] apiers wonse in thre munths, for he drinkes aile with Shadwell [Thomas Shadwell, poet and another of Charles II's boon companions] & Mr Haris [Joseph Harris, actor] at the Dukes house all day long. My Lord Burford [Nell's son by the king] remembers his sarvis to you. my Lord Bauclaire [Beauclerk, Nell's second son by the king] is goeing into france. We are goeing to supe with the king at whithall & my lady Harvie. the King remembers his sarvis to you. now lets talke of state affairs, for we never carried things so cunningly as now for we don't know whether we shall have peace or war, but I am for war and for no other reason but that you may come home. I have a thousand merry conseets, but I cant make her write um [possibly Nell is dictating this letter, and 'her' refers to the person taking the dictation, although the standard of spelling and grammar suggests perhaps Nell should have looked elsewhere for a secretary] & therefore you must take the will for the deed. god bye. Your most loueing obedunt faithfull & humbel sarvant E. [Eleanor] G.

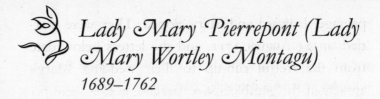

Lady Mary Pierrepont (Lady Mary Wortley Montagu)
1689–1762

Mary Pierrepont was the eldest child of Evelyn Pierrepont, later the first duke of Kingston-upon-Hull, and Lady Mary Feilding. Her mother died in 1692, having given birth to three more children; the siblings were then brought up by their paternal grandmother. When Mary was nine her grandmother died, and care of the children passed to her father. In later years Mary described herself as having 'stolen' her education in the library of his Nottinghamshire mansion, Thoresby Hall.

One of Mary's closest friends as a young woman was Anne Wortley, with whom she regularly corresponded. When Anne died in 1710, the correspondence was taken up by her brother, Edward Wortley Montagu, who soon asked her father's permission for Mary's hand. Permission was not granted because Pierrepont insisted on the entailment of Wortley Montagu's estate on his hypothetical first-born son, a practice with which Edward profoundly disagreed.

In August 1712, with Mary coming under increasing pressure from her father to marry the unsatirisably named Clotworthy Skeffington, the heir to an Irish peerage, Edward and Mary eloped. They were married on 23 August 1712, and the letters below date from the fretful run-up to their wedding. Mary's anxiety at the gamble she was taking is clear, and for the rest of her life she remained deeply grateful to her husband for marrying her without a dowry.

For the first two years of their marriage the couple lived in the country, and Mary gave birth to a son, also Edward, in May 1713. She was already writing poems and criticism, and became the first woman to have a contribution accepted by the *Spectator* magazine. In 1715, the Wortley Montagus moved to London and became important figures at the court of George I. Mary struck up friendships with politicians and members of the literati, including John Gay and Alexander Pope, who fell in love with her. In December that year, she barely survived a severe bout of smallpox, which left her permanently scarred.

In August 1716 Edward Wortley Montagu was posted as a diplomat to Constantinople in Turkey. The couple travelled out overland, the journey lasting about six months; Mary wrote many letters describing the fearsome undertaking, and kept copies with the intention of working them up into a book. In Turkey, she immersed herself in the local literature, culture, customs and religion, until her husband was unexpectedly recalled to London in July 1718, six months after Mary had given birth to a daughter.

After their return to England, Edward, frequently away on business in Yorkshire, bought houses in Twickenham and in Covent Garden, where Mary spent most of her time writing, gardening and overseeing the education of her daughter; she also wrote a series of poems about the oppression of women and edited her travel letters. She began a vicious feud with her former friend and admirer Alexander Pope, the reasons for which remain obscure. Her most important and lasting act during this time was to introduce the smallpox inoculation to England. She had come across it in Turkey, where inoculation with the live virus was a common practice. She had her son inoculated while they were there, and with a smallpox epidemic raging in England in 1721 she persuaded a doctor to inoculate her daughter. Soon, many of her acquaintances who had lost relatives to the disease were having their children inoculated too, and the practice became both increasingly widespread and endlessly controversial. Mary's evangelizing on behalf of inoculation led to her denunciation in the newspapers and even from the pulpit as an unnatural mother who risked the lives of her children to prove her crackpot theory, but Mary remained steadfast and encouraged other mothers to have their offspring inoculated against the disease that had nearly claimed her own life.

For the rest of her days Mary lived almost entirely apart from her husband. In 1736, she became infatuated with a brilliant young Venetian writer, Francesco Algarotti, and travelled to Italy in the hope of their having some kind of life together. For the next few years her movements were dictated by his whereabouts, and she spent time in Rome, Naples, Florence, Venice and Turin; she also lived for four years in Avignon, and for ten years in the Venetian province of Brescia, where she was more or less held captive by an upper-class bandit and thug named Ugolino Palazzi, who stole all her jewels and the title deeds to the property she had bought. When she returned to London in 1762, she had been abroad for the best part of thirty years; she died in Mayfair in August of that year, and is buried in the Grosvenor Chapel in South Audley Street.

Lady Mary Wortley Montagu undoubtedly had the capacity to become a great writer, but her work was so diverse in form – letters, journals, polemics, plays, poems, essays – and scattered in so many different places that its evaluation is still far from complete.

To Edward Wortley Montagu, 25 April 1710

I have this minute received your two letters. I know not how to direct you, whether to London or the country. 'Tis very likely you will never receive this. I hazard a great deal if it falls into other hands, and I write for all that.

I wish with all my soul I thought as you do; I endeavour to convince myself by your arguments, and am sorry my reason is so obstinate, not to be deluded into an opinion, that 'tis impossible a man can esteem a woman. I suppose I should then be very easy at your thoughts of me; I should thank you for the wit and beauty you give me, and not be angry at the follies and weaknesses; but, to my infinite affliction, I can believe neither one nor t'other.

One part of my character is not so good, nor t'other as bad as you fancy it. Should we ever live together, you would be disappointed both ways; you would find an easy equality of temper you do not expect, and a thousand faults you do not imagine.

You think, if you married me, I should be passionately fond of you one month, and of somebody else the next. Neither would happen. I can esteem, I can be a friend, but I don't know whether I can love. Expect all that is complaisant and easy, but never what is fond, in me. You judge a very wrong of my heart when you suppose me capable of views of interest, and that anything could oblige me to flatter anybody.

Was I the most indigent creature in the world, I should answer you as I do now, without adding or diminishing. I am incapable of art, and 'tis because I will not be capable of it. Could I deceive one minute, I should never regain my own good opinion, and who could bear to live with one they despised?

If you can resolve to live with a companion that will have all the deference due to your superiority of good sense, and that your proposals can be agreeable to those on whom I depend, I have nothing to say against them.

As to travelling, 'tis what I should do with great pleasure, and could easily quit London upon your account, but a retirement in the country is not so disagreeable to me, as I know a few months would make it tiresome to you. Where people are tied for life, 'tis their mutual interest not to grow weary of one another. If I had all the personal charms that I want, a face is too slight a foundation for happiness. You would be soon tired with seeing every day the same thing, where you saw nothing else. You would have leisure to remark all the defects, which would increase in proportion as the novelty lessened, which is always a great charm. I should have the displeasure of seeing a coldness, which tho' I could not reasonably blame you for, being involuntary, yet it would render me uneasy, and the more because I know a love may be revived, which absence, inconstancy or even infidelity has extinguished, but there is no returning from a degôut given by satiety.

I should not choose to live in a crowd. I could be very well pleased to be in London without making a great figure or seeing above eight or nine agreeable people. Apartments, table, etc. are things that never come into my head. But I will never think of any thing without the consent of my family, and advise you not to fancy a happiness in entire solitude, which you would find only fancy.

Make no answer to this. If you can like me on my own terms, 'tis not to me you must make your proposals. If not, to what purpose is our correspondence?

However, preserve me your friendship, which I think of with a great deal of pleasure and some vanity. If ever you see me married, I flatter my self you'll see a conduct you would not be sorry your wife should imitate.

To Edward Wortley Montagu, Friday night, 15 August 1712

I tremble for what we are doing. Are you sure you will love me for ever? Shall we never repent? I fear, and I hope. I foresee all that will happen on this occasion. I shall incense my family to the highest degree. The generality of the world will blame my conduct, and the relations and friends of ———— will invent a thousand stories of me. In this letter (which I am fond of) you promise me all that I wish. – Since I writ so far, I received your Friday letter. I will be only yours, and I will do what you please.

Postscript: You shall hear from me again tomorrow, not to contradict but to give some directions. My resolution is taken – love me and use me well.

Saturday morning, *16 August 1712*

I writ you a letter last night in some passion. I begin to fear again; I own myself a coward. – You made no reply to one part of my letter concerning my fortune. I am afraid you flatter yourself that my father may be at length reconciled and brought to reasonable terms. I am convinced by what I have often heard him say, speaking of other cases like this, he never will. The fortune he has engaged to give with me was settled, on my brother's marriage, on my sister and myself, but in such a manner that it was left in his power to give it all to either of us, or divide it as he thought fit. He has given it all to me. Nothing remains for my sister but the free bounty of my father from what he can save, which notwithstanding the greatness of his estate may be very little. Possibly after I have disobliged him so much, he may be glad to have her so easily provided for, with money already raised, especially if he has a design to marry himself, as I hear.

I do not speak this that you should not endeavour to come to terms with him, if you please, but I am fully per-suaded it will be to no purpose. He will have a very good answer to make, that I suffered this match to proceed, that I made him a very silly figure in it, that I have let him spend

£400 in wedding clothes, all which I saw without saying any thing. When I first pretended to oppose this match, he told me he was sure I had some other design in my head. I denied it with truth, but you see how little appearance there is of that truth. He proceeded with telling me that he would never enter into treaty with another man, etc., and that I should be sent immediately into the north, to stay there, and when he died he would only leave me an annuity of £400.

I had not courage to stand this vein, and I submitted to what he pleased. He will now object against me, why, since I intended to marry in this manner, I did not persist in my first resolution? that it would have been as easy for me to run away from Thoresby as from hence, and to what purpose did I put him and the gentleman I was to marry for Expense etc.? He will have a thousand plausible reasons for being irreconcilable, and 'tis very probable the world will be on his side. – Reflect now for the last time in what manner you must take me. I shall come to you with only a night-gown and petticoat, and this is all you will get with me.

I have told a lady of my friends what I intend to do. You will think her a very good friend when I tell you she has proffered to lend us her house, if we would come there the first night. I did not accept of this, till I had let you know it. If you think it more convenient to carry me to your lodging, make no scruple of it. Let it be what it will; if I am your wife, I shall think no place unfit for me where you are. I beg we may leave London next morning, where ever you intend to go. I should wish to go out of England if it suits with your affairs. You are the best judge of your father's temper. If you think it would be obliging to him, or necessary for you, I will go with you immediately to ask his pardon and his blessing. If that is not proper at first, I think the best scheme is going to the spa. When you come back you may endeavour to make your father admit of seeing me, and treat with mine (tho' I persist in thinking it will be to no purpose). But I cannot think of living in the midst of my relations and acquaintance after so unjustifiable a step – unjustifiable to the world. – But I think I can justify my self to my self.

I again beg you to hire a coach to be at the door early Monday morning to carry us some part of our way, wherever you resolve our journey shall be. If you determine to go to the lady's house, you had better come with a coach and six at 7 o'clock tomorrow. She and I will be in the balcony that looks on the road; you have nothing to do but to stop under it, and we will come down to you. Do in this what you like best. After all, think very seriously. Your letter which will be waited for, is to determine every thing. I forgive you a coarse expression in your last, which however I wish had not been there. You might have said something like it without expressing it in that manner, but there was so much complaisance in the rest of it, I ought to be satisfied. You can show me no goodness I shall not be sensible of. However, think again, and resolve never to think of me if you have the least doubt, or that it is likely to make you uneasy in your fortune. I believe to travel is the most likely way to make a solitude agreeable, and not tiresome. Remember you have promised it.

'Tis something odd for a woman that brings nothing to expect any thing, but after the way of my education I dare not pretend to live but in some degree suitable to it. I had rather die than return to a dependency upon relations I have disobliged. Save me from that fear if you love me. If you cannot, or think I ought not to expect it, be sincere and tell me so. 'Tis better I should not be yours at all, than for a short happiness involve my self in ages of misery. I hope there will never be occasion for this precaution but however 'tis necessary to make it. I depend entirely on your honour, and I cannot suspect you of any way doing wrong. Do not imagine I shall be angry at anything you can tell me. Let it be sincere. Do not impose on a woman that leaves all things for you.

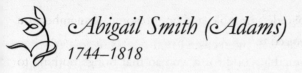

Abigail Smith (Adams)
1744–1818

Abigail Smith was born in Weymouth, Massachusetts, the daughter of William Smith, a minister, and Elizabeth Quincy, whose father was active in politics and government and was for forty years the Speaker of the Massachusetts Assembly. Abigail grew up without a formal education, but was encouraged by her father and her maternal grandfather to read widely in their extensive libraries.

She married John Adams, a Harvard lawyer, in 1764, and they settled on a farm near Adams' birthplace outside Boston while he built up his law practice in the city. It was in 1774, when John Adams went to Philadelphia to serve as the Massachusetts delegate to the First Continental Congress, that the couple embarked on a lifelong correspondence numbering more than 1,100 letters, which provides an invaluable portrait both of their marriage and the extraordinarily eventful times through which they lived.

John Adams, after serving in the Continental Congress and taking a large role in the drafting and defending of the Declaration of Independence, was posted to France and then Britain as the first US ambassador to the Court of St James; between 1778 and 1785 he was overseas a great deal. He and Abigail continued to write to each other despite the difficulties of a transatlantic correspondence; he kept her informed about the international situation, and she kept him apprised of how things stood at home, in both the governmental and the domestic spheres. Abigail joined him in 1783 and explored both Paris and London, where the couple were received by the king.

John Adams became the first vice-president of the United States in 1789, and was elected as its second president in 1797. Mr and Mrs Adams lived in the White House for only four months, from November 1800, during which time Abigail famously hung her family's laundry to dry in the unfinished East Room. She was regularly consulted by her husband on matters of policy – her influence led to her being criticized in the press and derisively referred to as 'Mrs President', a line of attack that remains wearisomely familiar. When the president was defeated for re-election by Thomas Jefferson, he and Abigail retired to Massachusetts, where they remained for the rest of their lives. Abigail died in 1818, six years before her son John Quincy Adams became the sixth president of the United States.

The letters below can give only a tiny flavour of the fascinating correspondence between this most devoted of couples. The second letter here was written as Congress was drafting the Declaration of Independence, and Abigail exhorts her husband to 'Remember the Ladies, and be more generous and favourable to them than your ancestors. Do not put such unlimited power into the hands of the Husbands. Remember all Men would be tyrants if they could.'

To John Adams
Sent from Braintree, 19 August 1774

The great distance between us, makes the time appear very long to me. It seems already a month since you left me. The great anxiety I feel for my Country, for you and for our family renders the day tedious, and the night unpleasent. The Rocks and quick Sands appear upon every Side. What course you can or will take is all wrapt in the Bosom of futurity. Uncertainty and expectation leave the mind great Scope. Did ever any Kingdom or State regain their Liberty, when once it was invaded without Blood shed? I cannot think of it without horror.

Yet we are told that all the Misfortunes of Sparta were occasiond by their too great Sollicitude for present tranquility, and by an excessive love of peace they neglected the means of making it sure and lasting. They ought to have reflected says Polibius that as there is nothing more desirable, or advantages than peace, when founded in justice and honour, so there is nothing more shameful and at the same time more pernicious when attained by bad measures, and purchased at the price of liberty. [. . .]

I have taken a very great fondness for reading Rollin's ancient History since you left me. I am determined to go thro with it if posible in these my days of solitude. I find great pleasure and entertainment from it, and I have perswaided Johnny to read me a page or two every day, and hope he will from his desire to oblige me entertain a fondness for it. – We have had a charming rain which lasted 12 hours and has greatly revived the dying fruits of the earth.

I want much to hear from you. I long impatiently to have you upon the Stage of action. The first of September or the month of September, perhaps may be of as much importance to Great Britan as the Ides of March were to Ceaser. I wish you every Publick as well, as private blessing, and that wisdom which is profitable both for instruction and edification to conduct you in this difficult day. – The little flock remember Pappa, and kindly wish to see him. So does your most affectionate

Abigail Adams

To John Adams
Sent from Braintree, 31 March 1776

I wish you would ever write me a Letter half as long as I write you; and tell me if you may where your Fleet are gone? What sort of Defence Virginia can make against our common Enemy? Whether it is so situated as to make an able Defence? Are not the Gentery Lords and the common people vassals, are they not like the uncivilized Natives Brittain represents us to be? I hope their Riffel Men who have shewen themselves very savage and even Blood thirsty; are not a specimen of the Generality of the people.

I am willing to allow the Colony great merrit for having produced a Washington but they have been shamefully duped by a Dunmore.

I have sometimes been ready to think that the passion for Liberty cannot be Eaquelly Strong in the Breasts of those who have been accustomed to deprive their fellow Creatures of theirs. Of this I am certain that it is not founded upon that generous and christian principal of doing to others as we would that others should do unto us.

Do not you want to see Boston; I am fearfull of the small pox, or I should have been in before this time. I got Mr. Crane to go to our House and see what state it was in. I find it has been occupied by one of the Doctors of a Regiment, very dirty, but no other damage has been done to it. The few things which were left in it are all gone. Cranch has the key which he never deliverd up. I have wrote to him for it and am determined to get it cleand as soon as possible and shut it up. I look upon it a new acquisition of property, a property which one month ago I did not value at a single Shilling, and could with pleasure have seen it in flames.

The Town in General is left in a better state than we expected, more oweing to a percipitate flight than any Regard to the inhabitants, tho some individuals discoverd a sense of honour and justice and have left the rent of the Houses in which they were, for the owners and the furniture unhurt, or if damaged suffcent to make it good.

Others have committed abominable Ravages. The Mansion House of your President is safe and the furniture unhurt whilst both the House and Furniture of the Solisiter General have fallen a prey to their own merciless party. Surely the very Fiends feel a Reverential awe for Virtue and patriotism, whilst they Detest the paricide and traitor.

I feel very differently at the approach of spring to what I did a month ago. We knew not then whether we could plant or sow with safety, whether when we had toild we could reap the fruits of our own industery, whether we could rest in our own Cottages, or whether we should not be driven from the sea coasts to seek shelter in the wilderness, but now we feel as if we might sit under our own vine and eat the good of the land.

I feel a gaieti de Coar to which before I was a stranger. I think the Sun looks brighter, the Birds sing more melodiously, and Nature puts on a more chearfull countanance. We feel a temporary peace, and the poor fugitives are returning to their deserted habitations.

Tho we felicitate ourselves, we sympathize with those who are trembling least the Lot of Boston should be theirs. But they cannot be in similar circumstances unless pusil-animity and cowardise should take possession of them. They have time and warning given them to see the Evil and shun it. – I long to hear that you have declared an independency – and by the way in the new Code of Laws which I suppose it will be necessary for you to make I desire you would Remember the Ladies, and be more generous and favourable to them than your ancestors. Do not put such unlimited power into the hands of the Husbands. Remember all Men would be tyrants if they could. If perticuliar care and atten-tion is not paid to the Laidies we are determined to foment a Rebelion, and will not hold ourselves bound by any Laws in which we have no voice, or Representation.

That your Sex are Naturally Tyrannical is a Truth so thoroughly established as to admit of no dispute, but such of you as wish to be happy willingly give up the harsh title of Master for the more tender and endearing one of Friend. Why then, not put it out of the power of the vicious and the Lawless to use us with cruelty and indignity with impunity. Men of Sense in all Ages abhor those customs which treat us only as the vassals of your Sex. Regard us then as Beings placed by providence under your protection and in immitation of the Supreem Being make use of that power only for our happiness.

To John Adams
Sent from Braintree, 5 April 1776

Not having an opportunity of sending this I shall add a few lines more; tho not with a heart so gay. I have been attending the sick chamber of our Neighbour Trot whose affliction I most sensibly feel but cannot discribe, striped of two lovely children in one week. Gorge the Eldest died on wedensday and Billy the youngest on fryday, with the Canker fever, a terible disorder so much like the throat distemper, that it differs but little from it. Betsy Cranch has been very bad, but upon the recovery. Becky Peck they do not expect will live out the day. Many grown persons are now sick with it, in this street 5. It rages much in other Towns. The Mumps too are very frequent. Isaac is now confined with it. Our own little flock are yet well. My Heart trembles with anxiety for them. God preserve them.

I want to hear much oftener from you than I do. March 8 was the last date of any that I have yet had. – You inquire of whether I am making Salt peter. I have not yet attempted it, but after Soap making believe I shall make the experiment. I find as much as I can do to manufacture cloathing for my family which would else be Naked. I know of but one person in this part of the Town who has made any, that is Mr. Tertias Bass as he is calld who has got very near an hundred weight which has been found to be very good. I have heard of some others in the other parishes. Mr. Reed of Weymouth has been applied to, to go to Andover to the mills which are now at work, and has gone. I have lately seen a small Manuscrip describing the proportions for the various sorts of powder, fit for cannon, small arms and pistols. If it would be of any Service your way I will get it transcribed and send it to you. – Every one of your Friends send their Regards, and all the little ones. Your Brothers youngest child lies bad with convulsion fitts. Adieu. I need not say how much I am Your ever faithfull Friend.

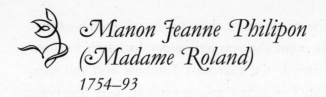

Manon Jeanne Philipon
(Madame Roland)
1754–93

Marie-Jeanne Philipon (known to her friends as
Manon) was the daughter of a Parisian engraver, and
even as a girl demonstrated a lively and enquiring
mind. She was mainly self-taught; the two biggest
influences on her life were probably the writings of
Plutarch and, latterly, Rousseau.

In 1781, Marie-Jeanne married Jean Roland de la
Platière, a manufacturing inspector who also wrote on
politics and economics and was a contributor to
Diderot's Encyclopaedia. The couple moved to Lyon,
where M. Roland contributed articles sympathetic to
the aims of the French Revolution to the regional
newspaper. In 1791 M. Roland went to Paris to appeal
for help for the Lyon silk industry, which was in crisis,
and became intimate with many key revolutionary figures; shortly afterwards, the couple moved there
permanently, and Mme Roland became the hostess of
a prominent political salon, which espoused the revolutionary cause.

With the declaration of the Republic in 1792, M.
Roland was appointed interior minister, but two days

after the execution of the king, he resigned his office. At this point the revolutionaries had split into two main camps, the extremist Jacobins and the more moderate Girondins amongst whom were numbered the Rolands. The Jacobins, led by Robespierre, staged a coup, which finally led to the Terror; the Girondins were summarily sentenced to death by guillotine by the Revolutionary Tribunal. Madame Roland helped her husband to flee, but she herself was arrested in June 1793 and tried on the charge of harbouring royalist sympathies. While in prison she wrote her memoirs, a document that charts the development of her intellect and her political thought and provides a fascinating history of the revolution. It also reveals Madame Roland's struggle to negotiate the path between her feelings about appropriate feminine behaviour and her gifts as a writer and intellectual.

On 8 November she was taken to the Place de la Revolution to be executed. On her way to the guillotine, she paused before the makeshift clay statue of Liberty that had been raised there and cried, 'O Liberty, what crimes are committed in thy name!' *Le Moniteur*, the revolutionary newspaper, published the following obituary: 'She was a mother, but had sacrificed nature by wishing to be above her station. The desire to be a learned woman led her to forget the virtues of her sex, and that omission, always dangerous, led her to die on the scaffold.' Her husband had escaped as far as Rouen, but on hearing of his wife's execution, he ran himself through with his sword by the side of a country road.

The letter below is to Léonard Buzot, the Rolands' fellow Girondin and possibly the lover of Madame Roland; he was on the run, but he too committed suicide in a Bordeaux forest that same year.

To Léonard Buzot
Sent from prison, 22 June 1793

How often do I not re-read your letters! I press them to my heart, I cover them with my kisses. I did not expect any more. Without success I asked for news of you from Madame Cholet. I wrote once to M. le Tellier in Evreux, so that you should receive a sign of life from me, but the postal connection is interrupted. I did not want to send you anything direct, because your name would suffice for the letter to be intercepted, and I might besides attract suspicion to you. Proud and calm I came here, with wishes for the defenders of liberty and some hopes for them. When I heard of the decree of arrest that had been promulgated against the twenty-two, I exclaimed 'My country is lost.' I remained in painful anxiety, before I had certain news of your flight, and the decree issued for your arrest frightens me anew. This horrible thing is no doubt due to your courage; since I know that you are in the Calvados, I regain my equanimity. Continue in your noble endeavours, my friend. Brutus despaired too soon of the Roman safety at the battle of Philippi. As long as a republican still breathes, is free, has his courage, he must, he can be useful. The south of France offers you in any case a refuge, and will be the asylum of honourable men. Thither you must turn your looks and wend your steps. There you will have to live, in order to serve your fellows and to exercise your virtues.

I personally shall know how to wait quietly, until the reign of justice returns, or shall undergo the last acts of violence, of tyranny in such a manner, that my example too will not be without utility . . .

Maria Smythe
(Mrs Fitzherbert)
1756–1837

Maria Anne Fitzherbert grew up in Hampshire, the daughter of a Walter Smythe, a former soldier, and his wife Mary Errington; both families were Catholic. At about twelve, she was sent to a Parisian convent for her education. She married and was widowed twice by 1781, leaving her a young woman of independent means.

The Prince of Wales, who was to become Prince Regent and eventually George IV, began his pursuit of her in 1784 after a chance meeting outside the opera house. She refused to become his mistress, and he eventually begged her to marry him, notwithstanding the three Acts of Parliament that stood in their way (the Act of Settlement, the Act of Union and the Royal Marriages Act). Mrs Fitzherbert declined his proposal and announced her intention to travel abroad. As a result the not notably restrained prince stabbed himself at his London home, Carlton House in Pall Mall, and dispatched his surgeon and three other friends to tell her that he would tear off his bandages unless she came immediately. She did, in company with Georgiana, Duchess of Devonshire, and the hysterical prince extracted from her a promise to marry him. She then left the country for Europe.

While she was away, the prince inundated her with letters, and although Mrs Fitzherbert regarded a promise made under such duress to be void, she eventually relented and agreed to marry him. The prince arranged the secret wedding, and in early November 1785 wrote her an impassioned forty-two-page letter; she returned to London the following month, and they were married in the drawing room of her house in Park Street on 15 December.

The prince then installed Mrs Fitzherbert in a house near his own in Pall Mall, but she was constantly exposed to insults and ridicule; speculation about the pair was feverish among their circle, in the press and in Parliament. There were (unfounded) hints that she was involved in a Catholic plot to destabilize the government. Another problem was the prince himself; he had managed to amass quite surreal debts as he turned Carlton House into a kind of fantasy palace, employing craftsmen from all over Europe, importing furniture from China and knocking down adjoining houses to make way for new wings. At one point, his treasurer, asked to calculate the money owed, professed it 'beyond all calculation whatever'. And, furthermore, he could not keep away from the ladies, despite the lengths to which he had gone to marry Mrs Fitzherbert. Eventually, the disapproving George III insisted that a suitable royal bride must be found for his wayward son, and the prince was more or less forced to marry Princess Caroline of Brunswick. In April 1795, exactly nine months after the wedding, Caroline gave birth to their only child, Princess Charlotte; by then, the couple were already living apart.

The prince and Mrs Fitzherbert were separated and reconciled several times up until 1811, when the rift became permanent; after this, the pair saw very little of each other. The prince's life became increasingly dissolute and scandalous; he was a gift to the caricaturists – immensely fat, painted and preening, drunk and gluttonous. Mrs Fitzherbert did write to him during his final illness in 1830; he was too ill to reply, but he died with a miniature of her around his neck, which was placed in his coffin. She died seven years later, at home in Brighton, discreet to the end.

To the Prince Regent

I was drawn to the Steine [a fashionable promenading area of Brighton] this evening by a party who drank tea with us and would not excuse me (though I was really too ill to go out) because it was generally believed that your —— —— [Royal Highness], in imitation of a ridiculous Frenchman, was to run a race backwards! Oh, that you had a mentor to guard you from those numerous perils that around you wait! The greatest of which are your present companions. As I beheld you the other day like another Harry:

> *Rise from the ground like feathered Mercury,*
> *and vaulted with such ease into your seat*
> *as if an angel dropt down from the clouds;*
> *to turn and wind a fiery Pegasus,*
> *and witch the world with noble horsemanship . . .*

I could not avoid continuing the comparison, and wish that you would sometimes use that Prince's words:

> *Reply not to me with a fool-born jest,*
> *for Heaven doth know, so shall the world perceive;*
> *That I have turned away from my former self,*
> *so will I those that kept me company.*

Adieu! If I am free to remember it is your own condescension that draws on you the remarks of

Margarita

To the Prince Regent

You will compel me to leave B*******, I am offended at your behaviour of last night. Why did I seek a walk retired? had we met on the Steine you would have been more guarded; alas! you have not the delicacy I wished! When you talk of love you offer an insult you are insensible of – your friendship confers honour; but your love – retain it for some worthy fair, born to the high honour of becoming your wife, and repine not that fate has placed my lot – in humble life. I am content with my station: content has charms that are not to be expressed. I know I am wrong in continuing this correspondence; – it must – it ought to cease: write therefore no more to

Margarita

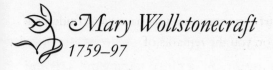

Mary Wollstonecraft
1759–97

Mary Wollstonecraft was born to a fairly well-to-do family in Spitalfields, east London, the second of seven children. Her father was, by her account, an alcoholic and a bully. Mary received scant formal education; her impressive learning was the result of her own self-discipline and determination.

By the time she reached adulthood, the family's means had dwindled to nothing, and Mary needed to earn a living. She worked unhappily as a teacher, a governess and a lady's companion before she took up writing, and in 1787 she published her first book, *Thoughts on the Education of Daughters*. Her publisher, Joseph Johnson, employed her to write essays for his magazine, the *Analytical Review*; he also became a life-long friend and mentor, and presumably a far more satisfactory paternal presence than her father had ever been.

Throughout the 1780s, Wollstonecraft lived the unremarkable life of a literary hack, although her appearance did raise some eyebrows: rough garments, worsted black stockings, unkempt hair which she refused to pin up. This early attempt to forge an identity which she felt was true to herself, rather than feminine convention (a precursor perhaps of the dungaree phase of twentieth-century feminism), was the beginning of a struggle which lasted her whole life.

Wollstonecraft's first big success came with her publication in 1790 of *A Vindication of the Rights of Men*, a riposte to Edmund Burke's post-revolutionary apologia for France's Ancien Régime. Mary was fêted as a leading radical, but she soon became frustrated with the lack of progress towards equal rights for women in this supposedly enlightened new age. She was inspired to write, in three months, her most celebrated work, *A Vindication of the Rights of Women*, which was published in 1792 and became an immediate international bestseller.

That same year, after an unhappy love affair with a married bisexual painter named Henry Fuseli (at one point, Mary had approached Fuseli's wife Sophia to propose a *ménage à trois* in which Mary would be recognized as Fuseli's 'spiritual spouse' – whatever that might have meant; a furious Sophia threw her out), Wollstonecraft travelled to Paris, where she met Captain Gilbert Imlay, an American soldier turned entrepreneur – handsome, charming and (inevitably) a well-known womanizer. By the end of 1793, Mary was pregnant, but after registering her as his wife at the

American embassy, Imlay disappeared on business. Abandoned and anxious, she followed him first to Le Havre, where her daughter Fanny was born in May 1794, and then to London, hoping to establish some kind of family life. Imlay did not share this ambition and was routinely unfaithful; the relationship dragged on until 1796. During that time she attempted suicide twice, once by swallowing a lethal dose of opium (she was rescued by a servant) and once by throwing herself into the Thames by Putney Bridge (she was pulled out by two passing boatmen).

After the final break from Imlay, Mary published *A Short Residence in Sweden, Norway and Denmark*, which she had written when she had travelled through Scandinavia, at Imlay's behest, in order to sort out some business affairs of his there. It was then she had realized there was no future to be had with Imlay, and this book, part memoir, part travelogue, part polemic, is her most personal.

Mary had first met William Godwin, the radical writer, in 1791, but it wasn't until 1796, when she took the bold (for the time) step of calling on him, ostensibly to lend him a book, that they fell deeply in love. By early 1797 Mary was pregnant and, despite the hostility both parties had expressed towards the institution of matrimony, they were married that March.

Their daughter, Mary Wollstonecraft Godwin, later Mary Shelley, was born on 30 August. Mary Wollstonecraft died of puerperal fever eleven days later. Her devastated husband wrote to a friend, 'I have not the least expectation that I can now ever know happiness again.'

In 1801, William Godwin married a neighbour, Mary Jane Vial, the mother of Claire Clairmont, whose letter to Byron appears elsewhere in this collection.

To Gilbert Imlay
Sent from Paris, Friday morning, 1793

I am glad to find that other people can be unreasonable as well as myself; for be it known to thee that I answered thy *first* letter the very night it reached me (Sunday), though thou couldst not receive it before Wednesday, because it was not sent off till the next day. There is a full, true, and particular account.

Yet I am not angry with thee, my love, for I think that it is a proof of stupidity, and likewise of a milk-and-water affection, which comes to the same thing when the temper is governed by a square and compass. There is nothing picturesque in the straight-lined equality, and the passions always give grace to the actions.

Recollection now makes my heart bound to thee; but it is

not to thy money-getting face, though I cannot be seriously displeased with the exertion which increases my esteem, or rather it is what I should have expected from thy character. No; I have thy honest countenance before me – relaxed by tenderness; a little – little wounded by my whims; and thy eyes glittering with sympathy. Thy lips then feel softer than soft, and I rest my cheek on thine, forgetting all the world. I have not left the hue of love out of the picture – the rosy glow; and fancy has spread it over my own cheeks, I believe, for I feel them burning, whilst a delicious tear trembles in my eye that would be all your own, if a grateful emotion directed to the Father of nature, who has made me thus alive to happiness, did not give more warmth to the sentiment it divides. I must pause a moment.

Need I tell you that I am tranquil after writing thus? I do not know why, but I have more confidence in your affection, when absent, than present; nay, I think that you must love me, for, in the sincerity of my heart let me say it, I believe I deserve your tenderness, because I am true, and have a degree of sensibility that you can see and relish.

Yours sincerely,
Mary

To Gilbert Imlay
Sent from Paris, evening, 23 September 1794

I have been playing and laughing with the little girl so long, that I cannot take up my pen to address you without emotion. Pressing her to my bosom, she looked so like you (entre nous, your best looks, for I do not admire your commercial face), every nerve seemed to vibrate to the touch, and I began to think that there was something in the assertion of man and wife being one – for you seemed to pervade my whole frame, quickening the beat of my heart, and lending me the sympathetic tears you excited.

Have I anything more to say to you? No; not for the present – the rest is all flown away; and indulging tenderness for you, I cannot now complain of some people here, who have ruffled my temper for two or three days past.

To William Godwin, 21 July 1796

I send you, as requested, the altered m.s. Had you called upon me yesterday I should have thanked you for your letter – and – perhaps, have told you that the sentence I *liked* best was the concluding one, where you tell me, that you were coming home, to depart *no more* – But now I am out of humour I mean to bottle up my kindness, unless something in your countenance, when I do see you, should make the cork fly out – whether I will or not –

Mary
Thursday
Judd Place West

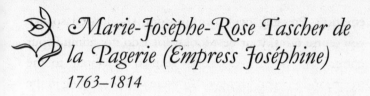

Marie-Josèphe-Rose Tascher de la Pagerie (Empress Joséphine)
1763–1814

Joséphine, as she was always called by Napoleon, was born in Martinique, the daughter of a wealthy plantation-owning family whose estates were destroyed by hurricanes in 1766. She left for Paris in 1779 to make an advantageous marriage to Alexandre, vicomte de Beauharnais, a French aristocrat. The marriage was not happy, although Joséphine bore him two children, Hortense and Eugène, before obtaining a legal separation in 1785. In 1788, she returned to Martinique, but left again for Paris in 1790 after a slave uprising on the island.

Joséphine led a glittering social life in Paris and maintained liaisons with several prominent men, but her life was endangered when her husband fell foul of the revolutionary Jacobins and was guillotined in June 1794. She was imprisoned, but was released after Robespierre himself was executed the following month. It was after her release and the establishment of the government of the Directory that she met Napoleon Bonaparte, a brilliant young army officer.

They were married in March 1796, just before

Napoleon left for Italy as commander of the French expedition. He wrote passionate love letters to her constantly, many of which survive, while there are very few surviving letters from Joséphine to her husband; either they were destroyed or they never existed. The latter explanation, it has to be said, seems the more likely one, as Joséphine was apparently a less than devoted wife, of dubious fidelity and tastes that ran from the merely expensive to the straightforwardly ruinous. Napoleon often complained bitterly both of her flirtations with other men and of her extravagance, and in 1799 threatened to divorce her; he was eventually persuaded against it by the intercession of her children by her first husband.

Napoleon's military and political success appeared unstoppable, and he was crowned Emperor of France in 1804 by Pope Pius VII (legend has it that he seized the crown from the Pope's hands at the moment of coronation and put it on his own head). He then crowned Joséphine Empress.

Joséphine's future now appeared secure: she was Empress of France, with her son married to the daughter of the king of Bavaria, and her daughter to Napoleon's brother. But her own marriage continued under strain, and in 1810 Napoleon was granted an annulment. Now he was Emperor he needed an heir, and with Joséphine unable to provide one he had set his sights on a dynastic marriage with the daughter of the Emperor of Austria.

Joséphine withdrew to the Château de Malmaison outside Paris, where she appears to have lived quite happily, entertaining her friends and protectors (who included Tsar Nicholas I) while remaining on good terms with Napoleon, who continued to pay her bills. The letter below dates from that time. She died of pneumonia four years later, and is buried in the nearby parish church of Reuil. The royal families of Holland, Luxembourg, Sweden, Belgium, Greece and Denmark are all descended from her. Napoleon's last words, when he died in exile on St Helena in 1821, were reported to be, 'France, the army, Joséphine.'

To Napoleon Bonaparte
Sent from Navarra, April 1810

A thousand, thousand tender thanks for not having forgotten me. My son has just brought me your letter. With what ardour I read it and yet I spent much time on it; for there was not a word in it that did not make me weep. But those tears were so sweet. I found again my whole heart, and such as it will always be; there are sentiments which are life itself, and which can only finish with it.

I would be in despair if my letter of the 19th had displeased you; I do not entirely remember its expressions, but I know what very painful sentiment had dictated it, it was the chagrin not to have had news from you.

I had written you at my departure from Malmaison; and since then, how many times did I not wish to write to you! But I felt the reason of your silence, and I feared to be importunate by a letter. Yours has been a balm for me. Be happy; be it as much as you deserve it; it is my entire heart that speaks to you. You also have just given me my share of happiness, and a share very vividly felt; nothing can equal the value for me of a mark of your remembrance.

Adieu, my friend; I thank you as tenderly as I shall always love you.

Joséphine

Mary Hutchinson (Wordsworth)
1782–1859

Mary Hutchinson married the great Romantic poet William Wordsworth in 1802; she was an old school friend of Wordsworth's sister, Dorothy, who until the marriage had been Wordsworth's principal companion. Dorothy recorded the wedding day in her journal:

On Monday 4 October 1802, my brother William was married to Mary Hutchinson. I slept a good deal of the night and rose fresh and well in the morning. At a little after 8 o'clock I saw them go down the avenue towards the Church. William had parted from me upstairs. I gave him the wedding ring – with how deep a blessing! I took it from my forefinger where I had worn it the whole of the night before – he slipped it again onto my finger and blessed me fervently. When they were absent my dear little Sara [Hutchinson, sister of the bride] prepared the breakfast. I kept myself as quiet as I could, but when I saw the two men running up the walk, coming to tell us it was over, I could stand it no longer and threw myself on the bed where I lay in stillness, neither hearing or seeing anything, till Sara came upstairs to me and said, 'They are coming.' This forced me from the bed where I lay and I moved I knew not how straight forward, faster than my strength could carry me till I met my beloved William and fell upon his bosom. He and John Hutchinson led me to the house and there I stayed to welcome my dear Mary.

So: on her wedding day, Mary Wordsworth had to look on with forbearance while her husband's sister managed to work herself up into a hysterical fit in which she was 'neither hearing or seeing anything', and then, in welcoming Mary to her new home, ensured that it was she who accompanied her brother over the threshold, rather than his bride.

Wordsworth's relationship with his sister and its influence on his work has been written about extensively; his relationship with his wife was barely even acknowledged until a cache of letters between Wordsworth and Mary were auctioned at Sotheby's in 1977. The letters revealed a marriage full of passion and affection, which is absolutely remarkable considering the circumstances of their domestic life. They were short of money; they shared their house with Dorothy and with Mary's sister, Sara, as well as an assortment of poets and critics including the increasingly drug-dependent nuisance that was Coleridge; and between 1803 and 1810, Mary gave birth to five children, two of whom died in 1812 plunging her into a deep depression. Later on life became slightly easier, as Wordsworth became more successful (he was appointed poet laureate in 1845), and the household moved to more spacious accommodation which afforded everyone more privacy, but the fact that the arrangements seem to have worked at all must be a testament to Mary's extraordinary patience.

In 1835, Dorothy was struck with some kind of pre-senile dementia; she was nursed by Mary for the last twenty years of her life. Wordsworth died in 1850; Mary outlived them both, dying in 1859. All three are buried in the churchyard at St Oswald's, Grasmere, in the Lake District, the landscape of which had provided Wordsworth with lifelong inspiration.

To William Wordsworth
Sent from Grasmere, Monday 1 August to Wednesday morning
3 August c.1810

O My William!
It is not in my power to tell thee how I have been affected by this dearest of all letters – it was so unexpected – so new a thing to see the breathing of thy inmost heart upon paper that I was quite overpowered, & now that I sit down to answer thee in the loneliness & depth of that love which unites us & which cannot be felt but by ourselves, I am so

agitated & my eyes are so bedimmed that I scarcely know how to proceed – I have brought my paper, after having laid my baby upon thy sacred pillow, into my own, into THY own room – & write from Sara's little Table, retired from the window which looks upon the lasses strewing out the hay to an uncertain Sun. – [. . .]

I look upon thy letter & I marvel how thou hast managed to write it so legibly, for there is not a word in it, that I could have a doubt about. But how is it that I have not received it sooner – It was written on *Sunday* before last – last Sunday *Morning* I rec^d. One of Dear Dorothy's written on the *Monday* & another in the evening of the same day, written on the *Thursday*; both *since* that day when my good angel put it into thy thoughts to make me so happy – Dorothy has asked me more than once when she has found me this morning with thy letter in my hand 'what I was crying about' – I told her that I was *so happy* – but she could not comprehend this. Indeed my love it has made me supremely blessed – it has given me a new feeling, for it is the first letter of love that has been exclusively my own – Wonder not then that I have been so affected by it.

Dearest William! I am sorry about thy eye – that it is not well before now, & I am SORRY for what causes in me such pious & exulting gladness – that you cannot fully enjoy your absence from me – indeed William I feel, I *have felt* that you cannot, but it overpowers me to be told it by your own pen *I* was much moved by the lines written with your hand in one of D's letters where you spoke of coming home thinking you 'would be of great use' to me – indeed my love thou wouldst but I did not *want thee* so much *then*, as I do now that our uncomfortableness is passed away – if you had been here, no *doubt* there would have existed in me that underconsciousness that I had my *all in all* about me – *that* feeling which I have never wanted since* the solitary night did not separate us, except in absence; but I had not then that leisure which I ought to have & which is necessary to be actively alive to so rich a possession & to the full enjoyment of it – I *do* William & I shall to the end of my life consider this sacrifice as a dear offering of thy love, I feel it to be such, & I am grateful to thee for it but I trust that it will be the last of the kind that we shall need to make –

* 'I slept with' was deleted

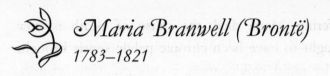

Maria Branwell (Brontë)
1783–1821

The mother of the great novelists Charlotte, Emily and Anne was born in Penzance, Cornwall, the eighth of eleven children. Her parents, Thomas Branwell and Anne Carne, were both from prosperous families, and were leading members of the Wesleyan Methodist community.

Both Maria's parents died when she was in her twenties. Her aunt, her father's sister Jane, invited Maria to join her at Rawdon near Leeds, where her husband, John Fennell, was the headmaster of a school, and in 1812 Maria left Penzance for a new life in Yorkshire.

Patrick Brontë, an old friend of John Fennell's, was the curate in a nearby parish, who met Maria when he visited Fennell's new school. The dates on the letters here demonstrate that the courtship between the two was short and intense; Patrick would regularly walk a round trip of twenty-four miles in order to take Maria for – a walk. By the end of the year, they were married.

Maria gave birth to six children between 1814 and 1820, the year the family moved to the famous parsonage at Howarth. The following year, after months of suffering, Maria died; the cause of death is now thought to have been chronic pelvic sepsis brought on by rapid childbearing, combined with anaemia. Four years later, her two elder daughters, Maria and Elizabeth, died of pulmonary tuberculosis contracted at the boarding school immortalized as Lowood by Charlotte in her fiction. By 1855, all the children had died, Charlotte and Emily having completed two of the greatest novels in the English language, *Jane Eyre* and *Wuthering Heights*. Patrick outlived them all, dying in 1861.

To Rev. Patrick Brontë, A.B., Hartshead
Sent from Wood House Grove, 26 August 1812

My dear Friend, This address is sufficient to convince you that I not only permit, but approve of yours to me – I do indeed consider you as my *friend*; yet when I consider how short a time I have had the pleasure of knowing you, I start at my own rashness, my heart fails, and did I not think that you would be disappointed and grieved, I believe I should be ready to spare myself the task of writing. Do not think I am so wavering as to repent of what I have already said. No, believe me, this will never be the case, unless you give me cause for it.

You need not fear that you have been mistaken in my

character. If I know anything of myself, I am incapable of making an ungenerous return to the smallest degree of kindness, much less to you whose attentions and conduct have been so particularly obliging. I will frankly confess that your behaviour and what I have seen and heard of your character has excited my warmest esteem and regard, and be assured you shall never have cause to repent of any confidence you may think proper to place in me, and that it will always be my endeavour to deserve the good opinion which you have formed, although human weakness may in some instances cause me to fall short. In giving you these assurances I do not depend upon my own strength, but I look to Him who has been my unerring guide through life, and in whose continued protection and assistance I confidently trust.

I thought on you much on Sunday, and feared you would not escape the rain. I hope you do not feel any bad effects from it? My cousin wrote you on Monday and expects this afternoon to be favoured with an answer. Your letter has caused me some foolish embarrassment, tho' in pity to my feelings they have been very sparing of their raillery.

I will now candidly answer your questions. The *politeness of others* can never make me forget your kind attentions, neither can *I walk our accustomed rounds* without thinking on you, and, why should I be ashamed to add, wishing for your presence. If you knew what were my feelings whilst writing this you would pity me. I wish to write the truth and give you satisfaction, yet fear to go too far, and exceed the bounds of propriety. But whatever I may say or write I will *never deceive* you, or *exceed the truth*. If you think I have not placed the *utmost confidence* in you, consider my situation, and ask yourself if I have not confided in you sufficiently, perhaps too much. I am very sorry that you will not have this till after tomorrow, but it was out of my power to write sooner. I rely on your goodness to pardon everything in this which may appear either too free or too stiff, and beg that you will consider me as a warm and faithful friend.

My uncle, aunt, and cousin unite in kind regards.

I must now conclude with again declaring myself to be Yours sincerely, Maria Branwell

To Rev. Patrick Brontë, A.B., Hartshead, 3 October 1812

How could my dear friend so cruelly disappoint me? Had he known how much I had set my heart on having a letter this afternoon, and how greatly I felt the disappointment when the bag arrived and I found there was nothing for me, I am sure he would not have permitted a little matter to hinder him. But whatever was the reason of your not writing, I cannot believe it to have been neglect or unkindness, therefore I do not in the least blame you, I only beg that in future you will judge of my feelings by your own, and if possible never let me expect a letter without receiving one . . . May I hope that there is now some intelligence on the way to me? or must my patience be tried till I see you on Wednesday? But what nonsense am I writing! Surely after this you can have no doubt that you possess all my heart. Two months ago I could not possibly have believed that you would ever engross so much of my thoughts and affections, and far less could I have thought that I should be so forward as to tell you so. I believe I must forbid you to come here again unless you can assure me that you will not steal any more of my regard . . .

I must now take my leave. I believe I need scarcely assure you that I am yours truly and very affectionately,

Maria Branwell

To Rev. Patrick Brontë, A.B., Hartshead, 21 October 1812

With the sincerest pleasure do I retire from company to converse with him whom I love beyond all others. Could my beloved friend see my heart he would then be convinced that the affection I bear him is not at all inferior to that which he feels for me – indeed I sometimes think that in truth and constancy it excels. But do not think from this that I entertain any suspicions of your sincerity – no, I firmly believe you to be sincere and generous, and doubt not in the least that you feel all you express. In return, I entreat that you will do me the justice to believe that you have not only a *very large portion* of my *affection* and *esteem*, but *all* that I am capable of feeling, and from henceforth measure my feelings by your own. Unless my love for you were very great how could I so contentedly give up my home and all my friends – a home I loved so much that I have often thought nothing could bribe me to renounce it for any great length of time together, and friends with whom I have been so long accustomed to share all the vicissitudes of joy and sorrow? Yet these have lost their weight, and though I cannot always think of them without a sigh, yet the anticipation of sharing with you all the pleasures and pains, the cares and anxieties of life, of contributing to your comfort and becoming the companion of your pilgrimage, is more delightful to me than any other prospect which this world can possibly present . . .

I should have been very glad to have had it in my power to lessen your fatigue and cheer your spirits by my exertions on Monday last. I will hope that this pleasure is still reserved for me. In general, I feel a calm confidence in the providential care and continued mercy of God, and when I consider His past deliverances and past favours I am led to wonder and adore. A sense of my small returns of love and gratitude to Him often abases me and makes me think I am little better than those who profess no religion. Pray for me, my dear friend, and rest assured that you possess a very, very large portion of the prayers, thoughts and heart of yours truly,

M. Branwell

Maria Bicknell (Constable)
1788–1828

Maria Bicknell met John Constable for the first time in 1800, when as a twelve-year-old child she came to East Bergholt in the Stour Valley to visit her grandfather, Durand Rhudde, the wealthy rector there. It wasn't until 1809 that Maria and Constable fell in love, but Durand Rhudde objected vehemently to the match, and threatened to disinherit not only his granddaughter, but her four siblings as well if it were allowed to proceed.

John Constable had lived in East Bergholt all his life, where his father was a merchant and mill owner. He loved painting and drawing from an early age, and escaped from the family business as soon as he could in order to pursue his artistic studies. In 1809, he was still a struggling young artist, committed to his vision of landscape painting (rather than the more lucrative portraiture), beginning to make some progress but still subsidized by family and friends.

For the next seven years, Maria and Constable managed their courtship through clandestine meetings and a secret correspondence, while Constable persevered with his artistic career. By 1816, despite Dr Rhudde's still implacable objection, Maria was persuaded that enough was enough, and the couple were married that October. (Dr Rhudde eventually softened sufficiently to bequeath her the same portion as her siblings when he died in 1819.) Despite Constable's dislike of portraiture, in July 1816, just after Maria had agreed finally to marry him, he executed a very touching likeness of her (now in the Tate collection), of which he wrote to her, 'I am sitting before your portrait – which when I look off the paper – is so extremely like that I can hardly help going up to it – I never had an idea before of the real pleasure that a portrait could afford.'

The obstacle to happiness in his personal life overcome, Constable's struggle to have his style of landscape painting accepted by the Academy, the critics and the public continued for decades. Maria's health was fragile, and she died of consumption in 1828, having given birth to seven children in eleven years. Constable was finally elected to full membership of the Academy three months later. He died in 1837; his paintings, many of which he refused to sell during his lifetime, now change hands for vast sums, and hang in galleries all over the world. His merits are still the subject of hot dispute.

My dear Sir, — I have just received my father's letter. It is precisely such a one as I expected, reasonable and kind; his only objection would be on the score of that necessary evil money. What can we do? I wish I had it, but wishes are vain: we must be wise, and leave off a correspondence that is not calculated to make us think less of each other. We have many painful trials required of us in this life, and we must learn to bear them with resignation. You will still be my friend, and I will be yours; then as such let me advise you to go into Suffolk, you cannot fail to be better there. I have written to papa, though I do not in conscience think that he can retract anything he has said, if so, I had better not write to you any more, at least till I can coin. We should both of us be bad subjects for poverty, should we not? Even painting would go on badly, it could hardly survive in domestic worry.

By a sedulous attention to your profession you will very much help to bestow calm on my mind . . . you will allow others to outstrip you, and then perhaps blame me. Exert yourself while it is yet in your power, the path of duty is alone the path of happiness . . . Believe me, I shall feel a more lasting pleasure in knowing that you are improving your time, than I should do while you were on a stolen march with me round the Park. Still I am not heroine enough to say, wish or mean that we should never meet. I know that to be impossible. But then, let us resolve it shall be but seldom; not as inclination, but as prudence shall dictate. Farewell, dearest John – may every blessing attend you, and in the interest I feel in your welfare, forgive the advice I have given you, who, I am sure, are better qualified to admonish me. Resolution is, I think, what we now stand most in need of, to refrain for a time, for our mutual good, from the society of each other.

To John Constable, *15 September 1816*

Papa is averse to everything I propose. If you please you may write to him; it will do neither good nor harm. I hope we are not going to do a very foolish thing . . . Once more, and for the last time! it is not too late to follow Papa's advice, and *wait*. Notwithstanding all I have been writing, whatever you deem best I do . . . This enchanting weather gives me spirits.

Claire Clairmont
1798–1879

Claire Clairmont grew up in a tangled household. Her mother, Mary Jane Vial, called herself Mrs Clairmont, although there is no evidence of her having been married; it is likely that Claire was illegitimate. Mary Jane was an enterprising woman who worked as a French translator and editor of children's books. A neighbour of the writer and political philosopher William Godwin, she became his second wife after the death in childbirth of his first, Mary Wollstonecraft. The household in north London contained five children, none of whom had two parents in common: Claire and her half-brother Charles; her stepsister Mary Godwin; Fanny Imlay, the daughter of Mary Wollstonecraft and Gilbert Imlay; and, from 1803, William Godwin, the son of Mary Jane and William.

In 1814 Mary Godwin, Claire's stepsister, eloped to Europe with Percy Bysshe Shelley, who was himself escaping from complicated and painful entanglements including a failed marriage. They were accompanied by Claire – an uneasy arrangement, one might think, and indeed for the rest of her life, Mary Shelley, as she became, was intermittently tormented by her husband's relationship with her stepsister. On her return to London, in 1816, Claire laid siege to the poet Byron, the celebrated author of *Childe Harold*, and the infamous womanizer and ne'er-do-well whose irresistible charisma and reckless behaviour terrified anxious mamas all over London. Claire appears to have had a plan, and that summer she contrived to engineer a meeting between Mary and Percy Shelley, Byron and herself at Lake Geneva. It was during this Geneva sojourn that the new friends spent an evening telling ghost stories, and Mary Shelley began *Frankenstein*.

In January 1817, back in England, Claire gave birth to Byron's daughter Allegra. Byron had by this time tired of Claire, but wished to maintain a relationship with his daughter, and in the summer of 1818 Claire allowed Allegra to be taken to him in Venice, after which Byron discouraged further contact between the child and her mother. After a complicated series of events – the usual Byronic cocktail of sex, scandal, domestic upheaval, political intrigue and boredom – Byron placed Allegra in a convent in Bagnacavallo, against Claire's wishes. Allegra died there, possibly of typhoid, at the age of four.

For the rest of her life, Claire Clairmont supported herself by travelling all over Europe as a governess and companion, much loved by her charges and her employers, despite having to conceal from them the radical connections of her past. She died peacefully in Florence at the age of eighty-nine, and is buried there; placed in her coffin was a shawl that had belonged to Shelley. Her bitterness towards Byron remained unmitigated.

To Lord Byron, 1816

You bid me write short to you and I have much to say. You also bade me believe that it was a fancy which made me cherish an attachment for you. It cannot be a fancy since you have been for the last year the object upon which every solitary moment led me to muse.

I do not expect you to love me, I am not worthy of your love. I feel you are superior, yet much to my surprise, more to my happiness, you betrayed passions I had believed no longer alive in your bosom. Shall I also have to ruefully experience the want of happiness? Shall I reject it when it is offered? I may appear to you imprudent, vicious; my opinions detestable, my theory depraved; but one thing, at least, time shall show you that I love gently and with affection, that I am incapable of anything approaching to the feeling of revenge or malice; I do assure you, your future will be mine, and everything you shall do or say, I shall not question.

Have you then any objection to the following plan? On

Thursday Evening we may go out of town together by some stage or mail about the distance of ten or twelve miles. There we shall be free and unknown; we can return early the following morning. I have arranged every thing here so that the slightest suspicion may not be excited. Pray do so with your people.

Will you admit me for two moments to settle with you there? Indeed I will not stay an instant after you tell me to go. Only so much may be said and done in a short time by an interview which writing cannot effect. Do what you will, or go where you will, refuse to see me and behave unkindly, I shall never forget you. I shall ever remember the gentleness of your manners and the wild originality of your countenance. Having been once seen, you are not to be forgotten. Perhaps this is the last time I shall ever address you. Once more, then, let me assure you that I am not ungrateful. In all things have you acted most honourably, and I am only provoked that the awkwardness of my manner and something like timidity has hitherto prevented my expressing it to you personally.

Clara Clairmont

Will you admit me now as I wait in Hamilton Place for your answer?

Jane Welsh (Carlyle)
1801–66

Jane Welsh was born in Haddington near Edinburgh in Scotland, an only child; her father was a doctor. Both her parents were Scottish. She was a precocious child with a lively, inquiring mind, and her father, whom she idolized, arranged for her to receive private tuition from the clergyman and scholar Edward Irving. When her father died in 1819, Jane was bereft. She had no occupation other than the fulfilment of social engagements and the manipulation of various suitors, including her former tutor, who unsuccessfully tried to break off his engagement to another woman in order to marry her. It was he who introduced her to the scholar and essayist Thomas Carlyle in 1821.

Carlyle was not considered a suitable match by Jane's mother, nor, incidentally, by Jane herself, but she valued his mind and his intellectual guidance. They were finally married in 1826. It seems that Jane saw her choice in fairly stark terms: she married Carlyle, who she regarded as a genius, in order to escape the stultifying life that otherwise awaited her in Haddington.

The Carlyles' marriage was tempestuous (the novelist Samuel Butler observed that it was 'very good of God to let Carlyle and Mrs Carlyle marry one another, and so make only two people miserable instead of four') and, while it lasted forty years, it is not even certain that it was ever consummated. Jane was an indispensable aid to her husband in his work, particularly when the almost completed manuscript of his history of the French Revolution was somehow put on the fire by the servant of a friend who had been reading it. Carlyle, with the steadfast encouragement of Jane, managed to reconstruct the whole thing.

For some time the Carlyles lived in Scotland, where Jane was lonely, isolated and miserable. It was when they moved to London in 1834 that she came into her own as a hostess, entertaining some of the most renowned writers, artists and politicians of the day, including Dickens, Thackeray and Tennyson. Her marriage encountered serious difficulty in 1843, when Thomas became infatuated with Lady Harriet Baring, who with her husband entertained in the grand style at their large house on Piccadilly or at their estate in the country. Jane, whose health was poor, drugged herself with morphine and struggled to understand how her gamble in marrying Carlyle had gone so badly wrong; she was now excluded from the circle in which she had shone, as Lady Harriet made it clear her invitations were extended to Thomas alone.

Lady Harriet died in 1857, and the final phase of the marriage was apparently happier and more tranquil than the rancour and resentment of the preceding decades. Jane Carlyle died in her carriage as she was being driven through Hyde Park in 1866. Her husband at once set to work on his *Reminiscences* and on a collection of her letters, with the avowed intention of winning for her the posthumous fame he felt she deserved. While his (possibly naive) frankness caused some scandal, his objective was largely achieved; her brilliance as a correspondent is widely recognized, and Jane Carlyle is routinely referred to as the best letter-writer in the English language. It is impossible to say whether or not, in a different time, she might have achieved success as an artist in her own right, but given her obvious talents, it is difficult not to speculate.

To Thomas Carlyle
Sent from Templand, Tuesday, 3 October 1826

Unkind that you are ever to suffer me to be cast down, when it is so easy a thing for you to lift me to the Seventh Heaven! my soul was darker than midnight when your pen said 'Let there be light,' and there *was* light at the bidding of the Word. And now I am resolved in spirit and even joyful, joyful even in the face of the dreaded ceremony, of *starvation*, and every possible fate.

Oh, my dearest Friend! be always *so* good to me, and I shall make the best and happiest Wife. When I read in your looks and words that you love me, I feel it in the deepest part of my soul; then I care not one jot for the whole Universe beside; but when you fly from my caresses to – smoke tobacco, or speak of me as a new *circumstance* of your lot, then indeed my 'heart is troubled about many things.'

My Mother is not come yet, but is expected this week; the week following must be given to her to take a last look at her Child; and then Dearest, God willing, I am your own for ever and ever . . .

Oh mercy! What I would give to be sitting in our doll's house married for a week! . . .

I may well return *one* out of *twenty*. But indeed, Dear, these kisses on paper are scarce worth keeping. You gave me one on my neck that night you were in such good-humour, and one on my lips on some forgotten occasion, that I would not part with for a hundred thousand paper ones. Perhaps some day or other, I shall get none of either sort; *sic transit gloria mundi* . . . And then not my will be done, but thine. I am going to be really a very meek-tempered Wife; indeed, I am begun to be meek-tempered already. My Aunt tells me, she could live for ever with *me*, without quarrelling – I am so reasonable and equal in my humour. There is something to gladden your heart withal! and more than this; my Grandfather observed while I was supping my porridge last night, that 'she was really a douce peaceable body that *Pen.*' So you perceive, my good Sir, the fault will be wholly your own, if we do not get on most harmoniously together . . . But I must stop. And this is my last Letter. What a thought! How terrible and yet full of bliss. You will love me for ever, will you not, my own Husband? and I will always be your true and affectionate

    Jane Welsh

To Thomas Carlyle
Sent from Liverpool, 2 July 1844

Indeed, dear, you look to be almost unhappy enough already! I do not want you to suffer physically, only morally, you understand, and to hear of your having to take coffee at night and all that gives me *no wicked satisfaction*, but makes me quite unhappy. It is curious how much more uncomfortable I feel without you, when it is I who am going away from you, and not, as it used to be, you gone away from me. I am always wondering since I came here how I can, even in my angriest mood, talk about leaving you for good and all; for to be sure, if I were to leave you today *on that principle*, I should need absolutely to go back tomorrow *to see how you were taking it.*

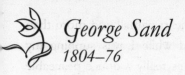

George Sand
1804–76

George Sand, the pseudonym of Amandine Aurore Lucile Dupin, was born to a well-to-do French family with a country estate in Nohant near the Indre Valley. She was married at nineteen to the Baron Casimir Dudevant, but the marriage was not a happy one, and at twenty-seven she left the baron and their two children and headed for Paris, where she fell in with a group of writers including the famous critic Saint-Beuve. She published her first novel, *Indiana*, in 1832, under the pen name of George Sand (an adaptation of the name of a lover and early collaborator named Jules Sandeau). The book was an outspoken critique of the inequities of the French marriage laws at the time, and a plea for women's education and equality.

People were scandalized by George Sand's cross-dressing, her smoking (it really didn't take much) and her many love affairs. She was an astonishingly prolific writer of novels, plays and essays, and while she attracted all kinds of opprobrium for her lifestyle, her appearance and her feminist and democratic beliefs, she was obviously a deeply attractive person.

One of her most celebrated love affairs was with the

poet Alfred de Musset, who was seven years her junior. He pursued her, declaring his love for her in a famous letter of 1833, when he was twenty-two and she was twenty-nine. George allowed herself to be persuaded, and they embarked on a trip to Italy; it is not entirely clear what transpired, but the enterprise was a disaster, and their relationship ended, messily, soon afterwards. What is known is that both George and de Musset were taken ill (there is speculation that de Musset's illness was a result of his predilection for the sometimes-lethal absinthe), and George, in a fit of romantic impetuosity, fell in love with their Venetian physician, Pietro Pagello. This relationship lasted no time at all; the letter to him below might explain why, particularly George's exhortation, 'Do not learn my language, and I shall not look for, in yours, words to express my doubts and my fears. I want to be ignorant of what you do with your life and what part you play among your fellow men. I do not even want to know your name.'

After many adventures, George Sand withdrew to her family's estate in Nohant, where she lived a more tranquil life, frequently visited by her many friends from her eventful past. She died there at the age of seventy-nine.

To Alfred de Musset, 15–17 April 1834

I was in a state of shocking anxiety, my dear angel, I did not receive any letter from Antonio. I had been at Vicenza, on purpose to learn how you had passed this first night. I only heard that you had passed through the town in the morning. Thus the sole news I had about you were the two lines you wrote to me from Padua, and I did not know what to think. Pagello told me that certainly, if you were ill, Antonio would have written us; but I know that letters get lost or remain six weeks on the way in this country. I was in despair. At last I got your letter from Geneva. Oh, how I thank you for it, my child! How kind it is and how it cheered me up! Is it really true that you are not ill, that you are strong, that you do not suffer? I fear all the time that out of affection you are exaggerating your good health. Oh, may God give it you and preserve you, my *cher petit*. That is as necessary for my life henceforth as your friendship. Without the one or the other, I cannot hope for a single good day for me.

Do not believe, do not believe, Alfred, that I could be happy with the thought of having lost your heart. That I have been your mistress or your mother, what does it matter? That I have inspired you with love or with friendship – that I have been happy or unhappy with you, all that changes nothing in the state of my mind, at present. I know that I love you and that is all. [three lines erased] To watch over you, to preserve you from all ill, from all contrariety, to surround you with distractions and pleasures, that is the need and the regret which

I feel since I have lost you. Why has so sweet a task and one which I should have performed with such joy become, little by little, so bitter, and then, all at once, impossible? What fatality has changed to poison the remedies that I proffered? How is it that I, who would have offered up all my blood to give you a night's rest and peace, have become for you a torment, a scourge, a spectre? When these atrocious memories besiege me (and at what hour do they leave me in peace?), I almost go mad. I moisten my pillow with tears. I hear your voice calling to me in the silence of the night. Who will call me now? Who will have need of my watching? How shall I use up my strength that I had accumulated for you, and that now turns against me? Oh, my child, my child? How much do I not need your tenderness and your pardon! Never ask me for mine, never say that you have done me wrong. How I do know? I don't remember anything, except that we have been very unhappy and that we have parted. But I know, I feel that we shall love each other all our lives from our heart, from our intelligence, that we shall endeavour, by a sacred affection [word erased] to cure ourselves mutually from the ills we have suffered for each other.

Alas, no! it was not our fault. We obeyed our destiny, for our characters, more impulsive than others', prevented us from acquiescing in the life of ordinary lovers. But we were born to know and to love each other, be sure of that. Had it not been for thy youth and the weakness which thy tears caused me, one morning, we should have remained brother and sister . . .

Thou art right, our embraces were an incest, but we did not know it. We threw ourselves innocently and sincerely into each other's arms. Well, then, have we had a single souvenir of these embraces which was not chaste and holy? Thou hast reproached me, on a day of fever and delirium, that I never made you feel the pleasures of love. I shed tears at that, and now I am well content that there has been something true in that speech. I am well content that these pleasures have been more austere, more veiled than those you will find elsewhere. At least you will not be reminded of me in the arms of other women. But when you are alone, when you feel the need to pray and to shed tears, you will think of your George, of your true comrade, of your sick-nurse, of your friend, of something better than that. For the sentiment which unites us is combined of so many things, that it can compare to none other. The world will never understand it at all. So much the better. We love each other, and we can snap our fingers at it . . .

Adieu, adieu, my dear little child. Write me very often, I beg of you. Oh that I knew you arrived in Paris safe and sound!

Remember that you have promised me to take care of yourself. Adieu, my Alfred, love your George.

Send me, I beg of you, twelve pairs of glacé gloves, six yellow and six of colour. Send me, above all, the verses you have made. All, I have not a single one!

To Pietro Pagello
Sent from Venice, 10 July 1834

Born under different skies we have neither the same thoughts nor the same language – have we, perhaps, hearts that resemble one another?

The mild and cloudy climate from which I come has left me with gentle and melancholy impressions; what passions has the generous sun that has bronzed your brow given you? I know how to love and how to suffer, and you, what do you know of love?

The ardour of your glances, the violent clasp of your arms, the fervour of your desire, tempt me and frighten me. I do not know whether to combat your passion or to share it. One does not love like this in my country; beside you I am no more than a pale statue that regards you with desire, with trouble, with astonishment. I do not know if you truly love me, I shall never know it. You can scarcely speak a few words of my language and I do not know enough of yours to enter into these subtle questions. Perhaps, even if I knew perfectly the language that you speak, I should not be able to make myself understood. The place where we have lived, the people that have taught us, are, doubtless, the reason that we have ideas, sentiments and needs, inexplicable one to the other. My feeble nature and your fiery temperament must produce very different thoughts. You must be ignorant of, or despise, the thousand trivial sufferings that so disturb me; you must laugh at what makes me weep. Perhaps you even do not know what tears are. Would you be for me a support or a master? Would you console me for the evils that I have endured before meeting you? Do you understand why I am sad? Do you understand compassion, patience, friendship? Perhaps you have been brought up in the idea that women have no souls. Do you think that they have? You are neither a Christian nor a Mussulman, neither civilised nor a barbarian – are you a man? What is there in that masculine bosom, behind that superb brow, those leonine eyes? Do you ever have a nobler, finer thought, a fraternal pious sentiment? When you sleep, do you dream that you are flying towards Heaven? When men wrong you do you still trust in God? Shall I be your companion or your slave? Do you desire me or love me? When your passion is satisfied will you thank me? When I have made you happy, will you know how to tell me so? Do you know what I am and does it trouble you not to know it? Am I for you an unknown being who must be sought for and dreamt of, or am I in your eyes a woman like those that fatten in harems? In your eyes, in which I think to see a divine spark, is there nothing but a lust such as these women inspire? Do you know that desire of the soul that time does not quench, that no excess deadens or wearies? When your mistress sleeps in your arms, do you stay awake to watch over her, to pray to God and to weep? Do the pleasures of love leave you breathless and brutalised or do they throw you into a divine ecstasy? Does your soul overcome your body when you leave the bosom of her whom you love? Ah, when I shall observe you withdrawn quiet, shall I know if you are thoughtful or at rest? When your glance is languishing will it be tenderness or lassitude? Perhaps you realise that I do not know you and that you do not know me. I know neither your past life, nor your character, nor what the men that know you think of you. Perhaps you are the first, perhaps the last among them. I love you without knowing if I can esteem you, I love you because you please me, and perhaps some day I shall be forced to hate you. If you were a man of my country, I should question you and you would understand me. But perhaps I should be still more unhappy, for you would mislead me. As it is, at least you will not deceive me, you will make no vain promises and false vows. You will love me as you understand love, as you can love. What I have sought for in vain in others, I shall not, perhaps, find in you, but I can always believe that you possess it. Those looks, those caresses of love that have always lied to me in others, you will allow me to interpret as I wish, without adding deceitful words to them. I shall be able to interpret your reveries and fill your silences with eloquence. I shall give to your actions the intentions that I wish them to have. When you look at me tenderly, I shall believe that your soul is gazing at mine; when you glance at heaven, I shall believe that your mind turns towards the eternity from which it sprang. Let us remain thus, do not learn my language, and I shall not look for, in yours, words to express my doubts and my fears. I want to be ignorant of what you do with your life and what part you play among your fellow men. I do not even want to know your name. Hide your soul from me that I may always believe it to be beautiful.

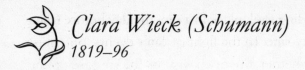

Clara Wieck (Schumann)
1819–96

Clara Wieck was born in Leipzig, daughter of the renowned piano teacher Friedrich Wieck and Marianne Tromlitz, a soprano and former pupil of Wieck's. Clara was a child prodigy, and her ambitious father devised a special programme for her, with daily lessons in piano, violin, singing, harmony, composition and counterpoint; she gave her first public recital in Leipzig at the age of nine. She first met her future husband, Robert Schumann, when he came to study with her father in 1830. Robert was a gifted pianist, but an injury to his hand meant that he could never fulfil his promise; instead, he became a composer and influential critic.

Clara toured Europe with her father between 1831 and 1835 and was also working on her own compositions. She was recognized as a virtuoso throughout France and Germany when Schumann began his courtship of her in the mid 1830s, and in 1837 he proposed marriage – below is her response. But Friedrich withheld his consent, and three years of bitter dispute followed. Eventually, the couple obtained permission from the Court of Appeals in Leipzig to marry, and their wedding took place in 1840, the day before Clara was twenty-one. In the light of later events, one must wonder whether Friedrich saw in the intense young man signs of the mental instability which would blight his later life. This was also the year that Robert composed more than a hundred of his famous *Lieder*.

Between 1841 and 1854, Clara Schumann gave birth to eight children, one of whom died in infancy. The family travelled all over Europe, with Clara show-casing Robert's compositions, and in 1850 they settled in Düsseldorf, where he became director of the city's orchestra.

Robert first suffered from depression and delu-sions in 1844; he recovered, but relapsed in 1854 and tried to drown himself in the Rhine while Clara was pregnant with their eighth child. He was rescued, but committed to an asylum, where he died two years later.

Clara survived her husband by forty years, bringing up her children alone, four of whom she also out-lived. For the rest of her life she taught, gave recitals all over Europe and devoted herself to burnishing her late husband's reputation as a composer. She gave her last public concert in 1891 at the age of seventy-two, and died after suffering a stroke in 1896.

It is only relatively recently that Clara Schumann's

own reputation as a composer has been re-evaluated; although she was writing music from an early age, she seemed to lose her confidence as she grew older, saying, 'I once believed that I possessed creative talent, but I have given up this idea; a woman must not desire to compose – there has never yet been one able to do it. Should I expect to be the one?'

To Robert Schumann
Sent from Leipzig, 15 August 1837

You require but a simple 'Yes'? Such a small word – but such an important one. But should not a heart so full of unutterable love as mine utter this little word with all its might? I do so and my innermost soul whispers always to you.

The sorrows of my heart, the many tears, could I depict them to you – oh no! Perhaps fate will ordain that we see each other soon and then – your intention seems risky to me and yet a loving heart does not take much count of dangers. But once again I say to you 'Yes'. Would God make my eighteenth birthday a day of woe? Oh no! that would be too horrible. Besides I have long felt 'it must be', nothing in the world shall persuade me to stray from what I think right and I will show my father that the youngest of hearts can also be steadfast in purpose.

Your Clara

Queen Victoria
1819–1901

Victoria was the only child of Edward, Duke of Kent, the fourth son of George III, and Princess Victoire of Saxe-Coburg-Saalfeld; her father died in 1820, and she was brought up in near isolation at Kensington Palace. She was permitted to know of her probable destiny at the age of ten – the occasion on which, according to legend, she exclaimed, 'I will be good!' She succeeded to the throne in 1837, when she was eighteen.

That same year Victoria was introduced to her cousin Prince Albert of Saxe-Coburg and Gotha, a match much wished for by her mother, but the new young queen was enjoying her first taste of independence, and in no hurry to change her circumstances. It wasn't until Albert presented himself again in 1839 that she fell in love with him. Victoria, as queen, had to propose to Albert, which must have been the occasion for some awkwardness, but he accepted and they were married on 10 February 1840.

Victoria's character – headstrong, stubborn, sociable – was transformed by marriage. Albert compensated for his wife's superior status with an absolute rule in the domestic sphere, and his punishment for wifely transgressions was a withdrawal of affection. Victoria, terrified of losing the husband upon whom she was increasingly reliant, would submit, and harmony would be restored. His letters, formerly addressed to 'Beloved Victoria', now began, 'Dear Child'. And of course the balance of power shifted as the couple began to reproduce; between 1840 and 1857 Victoria gave birth to nine children, all of whom, unusually for the time, survived to adulthood.

By the 1840s, Albert was joint monarch in all but name – and the fact that he had no official title was a constant source of fretful regret to Victoria. She tried in 1854 and again in 1856 to have him declared prince consort by Parliament; when her second attempt failed, she conferred the title upon him herself.

Albert was consulted by his wife in all matters of state, and she followed his direction. On his own account, he oversaw the construction of new royal homes at Balmoral in Scotland and Osborne House on the Isle of Wight, and supervised the triumphant Great Exhibition at Crystal Palace in 1851. It is impossible to overstate how much Victoria depended on her husband; her children were a distant second in her affections, and she would do nothing without his express approval. When he died in 1861, probably of stomach cancer, she was utterly inconsolable, and plunged the court into a mourning so deep as to be quite spectacular even by the stringent standards of the time. She declared, '*his* wishes—*his* plans—about everything, *his* views about *every* thing are to be *my law*! And no human power will make me swerve from what he decided and wished.' She did not emerge again into the public gaze until 1872, and even then it was only at the urging of her most senior advisers, who feared that republicanism was gaining a real foothold among the populace.

Victoria is a fascinating character: wilful yet entirely submissive to her husband; politically partisan to an alarming degree, but swayed by idiosyncratic personal likes and dislikes; avowedly anti-suffrage (having no truck with the '*socalled & most erroneous* "Rights of, Woman"', as she wrote to one of her prime ministers) yet wielding more power than any other woman in the world, and relishing the title of 'Victoria *regina et imperatrix*' (Victoria, queen and empress). She died in 1901, having celebrated her diamond jubilee. The queen believed it undignified to smile in portraits and photographs (much like today's Victoria *regina et imperatrix*, Mrs Beckham), and the image of the tiny (four foot eleven), dumpy, severe-looking woman swathed in black has become iconic, but there is a photograph taken in 1898 by Charles Knight in which she is caught off guard, smiling, and her entire aspect is transformed.

The first letter below was written to Albert ten days before their wedding. It reveals Victoria in her 'before' state, when she feels quite at ease asserting her authority over her husband-to-be; he has been lobbying for a long honeymoon in the country, and Victoria reminds him in no uncertain terms that her business lies in London. This state of affairs lasted a very short time indeed. The second letter, to her uncle King Leopold, gives some indication of her devastation after his death.

To Prince Albert
Sent from Buckingham Palace, 31 January 1840

... You have written to me in one of your letters about our stay at Windsor, but, dear Albert, you have not at all understood the matter. *You forget, my dearest Love, that I am the Sovereign, and that business can stop and wait for nothing. Parliament is sitting, and something occurs almost every day, for which I may be required, and it is quite impossible for me to be absent from London; therefore two or three days is already a long time to be absent. I am never easy a moment, if I am not on the spot, and see and hear what is going on, and everybody, including all my Aunts (who are very knowing in all these things), says I must come out after the second day, for, as I must be surrounded by my Court, I cannot keep alone. This is also my own wish in every way.*

Now as to the Arms: *as an English Prince you have no right, and Uncle Leopold had no right to quarter the English Arms, but the Sovereign has the power to allow it by Royal Command: this was done for Uncle Leopold by the Prince Regent, and I will do it again for you. But it can only be done by Royal Command.*

I will, therefore, without delay, have a seal engraved for you . . . I read in the newspaper that you, dear Albert, have received many Orders; also that the Queen of Spain will send you the Golden Fleece . . .

Farewell, dearest Albert, and think often of thy faithful
    Victoria R.

To the King of the Belgians
Sent from Osborne, 20 December 1861

MY *own* DEAREST, KINDEST *FATHER*, – For as such have I *ever* loved you! The poor fatherless baby of eight months is now the utterly broken-hearted and crushed widow of forty-two! My *life* as a *happy* one is *ended!* the world is gone for *me!* If I *must live* on (and I will do nothing to make me worse than I am), it is henceforth for our poor fatherless children – for my unhappy country, which has lost *all* in losing him – and in *only* doing what I know and *feel* he would wish, for he *is* near me – his spirit will guide and inspire me!

But oh! to be cut off in the prime of life – to see our pure, happy, quiet, domestic life, which *alone* enabled me to bear my *much* disliked position, CUT OFF at forty-two – when I *had* hoped with such instinctive certainty that God never *would* part us, and would let us grow old together (though *he* always talked of the shortness of life) – is *too awful*, too cruel! And yet it *must* be for *his* good, his happiness! His purity was too great, his aspiration *too high* for this poor, *miserable* world! His great soul is *now only* enjoying *that* for which it *was* worthy! And I will *not* envy him – only pray that *mine* may be perfected by it and fit to be with him eternally, for which blessed moment I earnestly long. Dearest, dearest Uncle, *how* kind of you to come! It will be an unspeakable *comfort*, and you *can do* much to tell people to do what they ought to do. As for my *own good, personal* servants – poor Phipps in particular – nothing can be more devoted, heart-broken as they are, and anxious only to live as *he* wished!

Good Alice has been and is wonderful.

The 26th will suit me perfectly. Ever your devoted, wretched Child,

Victoria R.

Emily Dickinson
1830–86

Emily Dickinson, one of the greatest poets of the nineteenth century, was born into a prominent Massachusetts family; her grandfather was a founder of Amherst College; her father was its treasurer and served in the General Court of Massachusetts, the State Senate and the House of Representatives. She had an elder brother, Austin, and a younger sister, Lavinia.

Emily was educated at Amherst Academy and then spent a year at the South Hadley Female Seminary, now Mount Holyoke College. In 1848 having spent just a year at the seminary, she returned to her family's house, known locally as the Homestead, where she lived for the rest of her life. Her only forays beyond Amherst were a trip to Washington, DC, to Philadelphia, and a few trips to Boston. She started writing poems in her early twenties, fitting her work around her domestic duties at the Homestead.

Emily Dickinson's withdrawal from all but her family's society seems to have been a gradual process, but it coincided with her most productive period as a poet in the early 1860s. Her most important literary mentor was Thomas Wentworth Higginson, a writer and radical. After he published an article giving advice to young writers in the *Atlantic* in 1862, Emily wrote to him enclosing some of her work. He was encouraging (if a little taken aback by what seemed to him the idiosyncratic style of the poems), and their correspondence lasted for the rest of her life (they met once, in Amherst, in 1870).

One of Emily Dickinson's closest relationships was with Susan Gilbert, whom she met as a girl at the Amherst Academy, and to whom she wrote more than three hundred letters. In 1856, after a four-year courtship, Susan married Emily's brother Austin, and the couple built a house next to the Homestead which they called the Evergreens. Their marriage was unhappy, but they lived there, together, for the rest of Emily's life.

Emily Dickinson's circumscribed existence in Amherst has left a sketchy biography – fertile ground for impertinent speculation and half-baked psychoanalysis. What is beyond dispute is that her reclusive life left her free to write almost 1,800 poems, only a handful of which were published before she died in 1886, but which eventually changed for ever the way people think about poetry.

After her death, more than forty 'fascicles' were

discovered in her room – manuscript books of poems that Emily had assembled and sewn herself. Various selections were published (some edited by Thomas Wentworth Higginson) between 1890 and 1935, but these versions were heavily reworked to conform with contemporary ideas about how poetry should look. It wasn't until 1955 that *The Poems of Emily Dickinson* appeared; edited by Thomas H. Johnson, it restored Emily Dickinson's revolutionary syntax, capitalization and punctuation, and finally revealed her true genius.

To Susan Gilbert (Dickinson), 6 February 1852

Will you let me come dear Susie – looking just as I do, my dress soiled and worn, my grand old apron, and my hair – Oh Susie, time would fail me to enumerate my appearance, yet I love you just as dearly as if I was e'er so fine, so you wont care, will you? I am so glad dear Susie – that our hearts are always clean, and always neat and lovely, so not to be ashamed. I have been hard at work this morning, and I ought to be working now – but I cannot deny myself the luxury of a minute or two with you.

The dishes may wait dear Susie – and the uncleared table stand, *them* I have always with me, but you, I have 'not always' – *why* Susie, Christ hath saints *manie* – and I have *few*, but thee – the angels shant have Susie – no – no no!

Vinnie is sewing away like a *fictitious* seamstress, and I half expect some knight will arrive at the door, confess himself a *nothing* in presence of her loveliness, and present his heart and hand as the only vestige of him worthy to be refused.

Vinnie and I have been talking about growing old, today. Vinnie thinks *twenty* must be a fearful position for one to occupy – I tell her I don't care if I am young or not, had as lief be thirty, and you, as most anything else. Vinnie expresses her sympathy at my 'sere and yellow leaf' and resumes her work, dear Susie, tell me how *you* feel – ar'nt there days in one's life when to be old dont seem a thing so sad –

I do feel gray and grim, this morning, and I feel it would be a comfort to have a piping voice, and broken back, and scare little children. Dont *you* run, Susie dear, for I wont do any harm, and I do love you dearly tho' I do feel so frightful.

Oh my darling one, how long you wander from me, how weary I grow of waiting and looking, and calling for you; sometimes I shut my eyes, and shut my heart towards you, and try hard to forget you because you grieve me so, but you'll never go away, Oh you never will – say, Susie, promise me again, and I will smile faintly – and take up my little cross again of sad – *sad* separation. How vain it seems to *write*, when one knows how to feel – how much more near and dear to sit beside you, talk with you, hear the tones of your voice; so hard to 'deny thyself, and take up thy cross, and follow me' – give me strength, Susie, write me of hope and love, and of hearts that *endured*, and great was their reward of 'Our Father who art in Heaven'. I don't know how I shall bear it, when the gentle spring comes; if she should come and see me and talk to me of you, Oh it would surely kill me! While the frost clings to the windows, and the World is stern and drear; this absence is easier; the *Earth* mourns too, for all her little birds; but when they all come back again, and she sings and is so merry – pray what will become of me? Susie, forgive me, forget all what I say, get some sweet little scholar to read a gentle hymn, about Bethleem and Mary, and you will sleep on sweetly and have as peaceful dreams, as if I had never written you all these ugly things. Never mind the letter Susie, I wont be angry with you if you don't give me any at all – for I know how busy you are, and how little of that dear strength remains when it is evening, with which to think and write. Only *want* to write me, only sometimes sigh that you are far from me, and that will do, Susie! Dont you think we are good and patient, to let you go so long; and don't we think you're a darling, a real beautiful hero, to toil for people, and teach them, and leave your own dear home? Because we pine and repine, dont think we forget the precious patriot at war in other lands! Never be mournful Susie – be happy and have cheer, for how many of the long days have gone away since I wrote you – and it is almost noon, and soon the night will come, and then there is one less day of the long pilgrimage. Mattie is very smart, talks of you *much*, my darling; I must leave you now – 'one little hour of Heaven,' thank who did give it me, and will he also grant me one longer and *more* when it shall please his love – bring Susie home, ie! Love always, and ever, and true!

    Emily

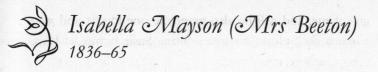

Isabella Mayson (Mrs Beeton)
1836–65

Isabella Mayson was born off Cheapside in the City of London, the eldest of four children. Her father, Benjamin Mayson, a linen merchant, died when she was four, and in 1843 her mother, Elizabeth, married Henry Dorling, who was the Clerk of the Course at Epsom. Henry was a widower with four children, so the couple began married life with a brood of eight; to this were added a further, scarcely credible, thirteen children over the next twenty years, making Isabella the eldest of twenty-one siblings, half-siblings and step-siblings. It is hardly surprising that she became a dab hand at household management.

Isabella was educated in Heidelberg, where her studies focused on music and languages, and where she also discovered her skill as a pastry chef, which she continued to practise for an Epsom confectioner when she returned there in 1854.

In 1856, Isabella married Samuel Orchart Beeton, a book and magazine publisher who had had an early success with the publication of *Uncle Tom's Cabin* by the abolitionist Harriet Beecher Stowe. Among Samuel's stable of periodicals was the *English Woman's*

Domestic Magazine, a twopenny monthly. Mrs Beeton became active in her husband's business almost straight away, and by 1859 was 'editress' of the *Domestic Magazine*. She was a great innovator – she returned from a visit to Paris with the idea of including a fashion plate in each issue, and a pattern service for readers; these features became staples of women's magazines for the next century.

The achievement for which Mrs Beeton's name is renowned was of course *Mrs Beeton's Book of Household Management*, which was published as a part-work between 1859 and 1861, then as an illustrated volume, followed by numerous mass-market editions. Mrs Beeton set out her stall in her introduction: 'I have always thought that there is no more fruitful source of family discontent than a housewife's badly-cooked dinners and untidy ways.' Aimed at the emerging Victorian middle class, *Household Management* was much, much more than a collection of recipes; it covered every aspect of the domestic sphere, including budgeting, the management of servants, etiquette (on finger bowls: 'The French and other continentals have a habit of gargling the mouth; but it is a custom which no English gentlewoman should, in the slightest degree, imitate'), hygiene, dress, first aid, childcare and even legal matters pertaining to buying a house, taking a tenancy, letting and insuring property and the drawing up of a will. *Household Management* is a monumental work, which now provides a riveting picture of middle-class Victorian women's lives; for its original readers though, especially newly married women, it must have been an absolutely indispensable guide to navigating all aspects of everyday life.

During the time that Isabella was compiling *Household Management*, she gave birth to four sons, two of whom died: one in his first year, the other at the age of three. Isabella died of peritonitis and puerperal fever eight days after giving birth to her fourth son, Mayson, in February 1865 at the terribly young age of twenty-eight. Samuel outlived her by only twelve years, succumbing to tuberculosis at the age of forty-seven. That his happy and immensely productive partnership with his wife lasted only eight and a half years, coupled with the death of their first two children, must have been a source of immense sadness to him.

My own darling Sam,

As I have two or three little matters in your note of yester-day that rather puzzled me, I thought I must write and ask an explanation; very stupid of me you will say, as I am going to see you on Wednesday morning. No doubt you will think that I could just as well have [asked you] myself then, as trouble you with one of my unintelligible epistles . . .

Secondly, what right has he to conjure up in his fertile brain such nasty things as rough corners to smooth down when there is one who loves him better and more fondly than ever one being did another, on this earth at least.

Oh Sam, I think it is so wrong of you to fancy such dreadful things. You say also you don't think I shall be able to guide myself when I am left to my own exertions. I must say, I have always looked up to, and respected, both parents and perhaps been mindful of what they say (I mean respect-ing certain matters) but in a very short time you will have the entire management of me and I can assure you that you will find in me a most docile and yielding pupil.

Pray don't imagine when I am yours – that things will continue as they are now. God forbid. Better would it be to put an end to this matter altogether if we thought there was the slightest possibility of *that*. So pray don't tremble for our future happiness.

Look at things in a more rosy point of view and I have

no doubt with the love *I am sure* there is existing between us, we shall get on as merrily as crickets with only an occasionally sharp point to soften down and not as many as you fancy . . .

I could not sleep without writing to you, so you must excuse this nonsense. Good-night my precious pet, may angels guide and watch over you and give you pleasant dreams, not drab colours, and accept the fondest and most sincere love of your

Bella

Burn this as soon as read.

Mary Wyndham (Lady Elcho)
1862–1937

Mary Wyndham was born in Belgravia into a family both aristocratic and artistic; her father was a patron of the pre-Raphaelites, and the family home was filled with painters, poets and writers. She was educated at home by a governess, and in 1883 the stunningly beautiful young woman (she was painted by both Edward Poynder and Sargent) was persuaded by her family to marry Hugo Richard Charteris, Lord Elcho. Charteris was a charmer, but a wastrel; the marriage was not happy, and Mary was often left alone with the children (seven were born between 1884 and 1902). But while she had failed to fall in love with Hugo, she had fallen in love with the house her father-in-law gave them as a wedding present: Stanway, in Gloucestershire, a fine Jacobean manor built of honey-coloured Cotswold stone, surrounded by beautiful grounds containing a spectacular eighteenth-century water garden and a fourteenth-century tithe barn. The house became a focal point for all sorts of gatherings – Mary was one of the legendary hostesses of the age – but most particularly the unofficial headquarters of a group that became known as 'the Souls'. In some ways a precursor to the Bloomsbury set, the Souls eschewed the usual aristocratic pastimes – tramping about shooting things and a fanatical interest in horse racing – in favour of conversation, music and word games. One of its leading lights was Arthur Balfour, then a backbench Unionist MP, who later became prime minister.

Balfour never married, and doesn't appear to have been particularly interested in sex. But the languid, intellectual and usually uncommunicative philosopher-politician found in Mary someone in whom he could confide; she in turn found the kindred spirit her husband clearly was not. Margot Asquith, a fellow Soul, claimed that Balfour was never in love, citing as evidence his response when she asked him if he would mind if she, Mary and another of their friends were all to die: 'I would mind if you all died on the same *day*.'

The friendship and correspondence between Mary and Balfour lasted for forty years until his death in 1930. She was evidently a woman of energy and wit, who for most of her life was locked in a loveless marriage, although in 1895 she embarked on an adventure to Egypt where she had an affair with the explorer Wilfrid Scawen Blunt and returned pregnant – her husband accepted the child as his own in keeping with the aristocratic custom of the time. In 1914 Hugo inherited his father's title and grand estate in East Lothian, where he decamped to live in splendour with his mistress. Mary managed to stay on at Stanway only through the charity of the playwright James Barrie. She lost two sons in the First World War, and as a memorial she wrote the story of their lives, *A Family Record*, which was published in 1932. Mary Charteris lived out her days at Stanway, and died in a nearby nursing home in 1937.

To Arthur Balfour
Written on a train between Oxford and Warwick,
19 January 1904

I was overwhelmed with depression at leaving you Sunday night, and I think you looked rather sad too which – this sounds unkind – was rather a consolation. It was horrid leaving at that hour but practically it was unavoidable so 'there's nothing to regret' in *that* sense (this is a Whitt phrase) except that it had to be done and I think it was quite clever of me to fit in everything so well and manage to get to you – you see, I felt it my duty to put you in *yr place* (on yr knees at my feet) and *that* I flatter myself I have thoroughly done. Sunday was a little disappointing, because altho' my conscience wanted you to go to church I *should* have liked to have had some fun with you in the morning. I was in great spirits and full of mischief when you rushed in. (by the way, how *awful* of you to leave my letter in yr room) then came the long walk and one hour in yr room seemed very little in all the day and it was wasted in talking business. 2 hrs is what I like: one for boring things and one for putting you in yr place: I know I dwell too much on each thing and the more I fancy you're bored the more gingerly I go, which is quite wrong. I hate rushing but it ought to be done as time is short. Then the interval between tea and dinner and departure was a great strain because I felt I wanted so to see you alone and kept *wondering* if it could be managed, certainly not unless I had arranged it beforehand – impossible to get yr attention, I thought of yr showing me something or fetching something in yr room. Eventually I gave it up and mental and physical spirits went down like a pricked balloon. I had some of my pain in my side. The motor drive was very nice but not so much fun *going away* in it. I tipped Mills . . .

I wish I had a motor. I forgot to tell you that Tuesday 6th would suit me best: I should like a clear week at Stanway but you must settle what pleases you.

Goodbye. Bless you.

ME

I hope you are all right? Destroy.

Edith Newbold Jones (Wharton)
1862–1937

Edith Wharton was born Edith Newbold Jones to a prominent New York society family who had made their fortune in shipping, banking and real estate. She was brought up in a brownstone on 23rd Street, just off Park Avenue, and was educated by governesses and by reading in her father's library. Edith seems to have been a born storyteller, and had completed her first (never published) novel by the age of fifteen.

Her mother, Lucretia, a doyenne of grand New York society, was anxious that this clever, bookish daughter find a husband; in 1885, she married Edward 'Teddy' Robbins Wharton, a friend of her brother's. A Bostonian, Teddy shared the moneyed, leisured lifestyle of his new wife's family, but sadly he had nothing at all in common with his wife in terms of temperament or interests.

Edith Wharton's struggle to reconcile her position as a society matron with her creative impulse meant that after her youthful flurry of productivity, she produced no further fiction until she was thirty-eight. In the meantime, her annual trips to Europe inspired her to write about art, architecture, gardens and interior design. Her first published book was *The Decoration of Houses*, co-written with the designer Ogden Codman, an argument in favour of a more classically elegant, restrained and simple style than the prevailing fashion for mammoth furnishings, dark colour schemes and clutter.

Her first bestselling novel, *The House of Mirth*, about the old New York society in which she had grown up, was published in 1905. Edith was by then living for most of the year in western Massachusetts in a classical villa of her own design called the Mount, while Teddy Wharton appeared to be increasingly in the grip of mental illness. A friend of Edith's wrote, 'Mr Wharton's mania leads him to buy houses and motors for music-hall actresses, to engage huge suites in hotels and get drunk and break all the furniture and to circulate horrible tales about his wife.'

In 1907, Henry James, who had become Edith's close friend, introduced her to Morton Fullerton, a Bostonian who had become Paris correspondent for the London *Times*. She fell in love with him and moved to Paris full time. Again she had chosen badly; Fullerton was a bisexual divorcé who was being blackmailed by a former mistress over his homosexual past and was involved in a quasi-incestuous affair with his cousin, who had grown up in his parents' household.

Teddy at least had the excuse of mental disorder for his appalling behaviour; Fullerton appears to have been an out-and-out opportunist, more or less a living definition of the word 'cad'. The affair between Edith and Fullerton lasted on and off until 1911. It is possible that when Fullerton realized Edith was moving towards divorcing the increasingly erratic Teddy, he thought it expedient to back off.

For the rest of her life Edith lived in France. She received the Legion of Honour for her war work, raising funds and establishing hostels for French and Belgian refugees, and also became a war correspondent, reporting from the front line back to the United States. In 1921, she received a Pulitzer Prize for *The Age of Innocence*, and in 1923 took an honorary doctorate in letters from Yale University. In 1930 she was elected to the American Academy of Arts and Letters. She died in 1937 at her house in Pavillon Colombe, just north of Paris. She is often described as a 'society novelist' or 'a novelist of manners' – both phrases carry with them a hint of the pejorative. She was an astonishingly astute and open-minded writer with a forensic eye for human fallibility, whose themes and interests ranged far beyond the drawing rooms of Old New York.

Dear, Remember, please, how impatient & anxious I shall be to know the sequel of the Bell letter . . .

—Do you know what I was thinking last night, when you asked me, & I couldn't tell you? —Only that the way you've spent your emotional life, while I've – bien malgré moi – hoarded mine, is what puts the great gulf between us, & sets us not only on opposite shores, but at hopelessly distant points of our respective shores . . . Do you see what I mean?

And I'm so afraid that the treasures I long to unpack for you, that have come to me in magic ships from enchanted islands, are only, to you, the old familiar red calico & beads of the clever trader who has had dealings in every latitude, & knows just what to carry in the hold to please the simple native – I'm so afraid of this, that often & often I stuff my shining treasures back into their box, lest I should see you smiling at them!

Well! And if you do? It's *your* loss, after all! And if you can't come into the room without my feeling all over me a ripple of flame, & if, wherever you touch me, a heart beats under your touch, & if, when you hold me, & I don't speak, it's because all the words in me seem to have become throbbing pulses, & all my thoughts are a great golden blur – why should I be afraid of your smiling at me, when I can turn the beads & calico back into such beauty– ?

Rosa Luxemburg
1871–1919

Rosa Luxemburg was born in Zamość, near Lublin, in Russian-controlled Poland, the fifth child of a timber merchant. She was educated in Poland and in 1886 joined the Polish Proletariat Party. By 1889, she was so notorious as a political agitator that she had to flee from Poland to Zürich, Switzerland, to escape imprisonment. She continued her studies at the University of Zürich, taking her doctorate in 1898. It was there that she met Leo Jogiches, with whom she founded the Social Democratic Party of the Kingdom of Poland. Rosa and Leo had a long love affair but never really lived together; their politics were, ultimately, more important to both of them than domestic happiness.

In 1898 Rosa married Karl Lübeck, the son of a friend, in order to move to Berlin. The two main strands of her political thought can be identified as a scepticism about nationalism – her cause was social-ist revolution across Europe, rather than individual nations acting alone – and a conviction that revolution, not reform, was the only way of bringing freedom to the masses.

Once in Germany, Rosa began agitating against

German militarism and imperialism and constantly found herself in trouble with the authorities, often for inciting mass strike action. In June 1916, as she tried to lead an anti-war strike, she was arrested and imprisoned for two and a half years. When the authorities reluctantly released her in 1918, she and her comrades immediately founded the German Communist Party and a newspaper called the *Red Flag*. In January 1919, amid scenes of revolutionary chaos in Berlin, Rosa was arrested by the so-called *Freikorps*, bands of paramilitaries associated with the right-wing movements which were beginning to gather momentum. She was taken to a hotel and beaten until she was unconscious; her body was then dumped in the Landwehr Canal. Her murder has been described as the first triumph of Nazi Germany.

The letter below to Leo Jogiches contains arguably one of the most poignant (and, it must be said, amusing) effusions in this collection: thanking him for the gift of a book, Rosa writes, 'You simply cannot imagine how pleased I am with your choice. Why, Rodbertus is simply my favourite economist.' (Rodbertus worked primarily on the labour theory of value.) This might go some way towards illustrating how the relationship between Luxemburg and Jogiches never became the first priority for either of

them, despite the love they may have felt for each
other.

To Leo Jogiches, 6 March 1899

I kiss you a thousand times for your dearest letter and present, though I have not yet received it . . . You simply cannot
imagine how pleased I am with your choice. Why, Rodbertus is simply my favourite economist and I can read him a
hundred times for sheer intellectual pleasure . . . My dear,
how you delighted me with your letter. I have read it six
times from beginning to end. So, you are really pleased with
me. You write that perhaps I only know inside me that
somewhere there is a man who belongs to me! Don't you
know that everything I do is always done with you in mind:
when I write an article my first thought is – will this cause
you pleasure – and when I have days when I doubt my own
strength and cannot work, my only fear is what effect this
will have on you, that it might disappoint you. When I have
proof of success, like a letter from Kautsky, this is simply
my homage to you. I give you my word, as I loved my
mother, that I am personally quite indifferent to what
Kautsky writes. I was only pleased with it because I wrote
it with your eyes and felt how much pleasure it would
give you.

   . . . Only one thing nags at my contentment: the outward
arrangements of your life and of our relationship. I feel that

I will soon have such an established position (morally) that we will be able to live together quite calmly, openly, as husband and wife. I am sure you understand this yourself. I am happy that the problem of your citizenship is at last coming to an end and that you are working energetically at your doctorate. I can feel from your recent letters that you are in a very good mood to work . . .

Do you think that I do not feel your value, that whenever the call to arms is sounded you always stand by me with help and encourage me to work – forgetting all the rows and all my neglect!

. . . You have no idea with what joy and desire I wait for every letter from you because each one brings me so much strength and happiness and encourages me to live.

I was happiest of all with that part of your letter where you write that we are both young and can still arrange our personal life. Oh darling, how I long that you may fulfil your promise . . . Our own little room, our furniture, a library of our own, quiet and regular work, walks together, an opera from time to time, a small – very small – circle of intimate friends who can sometimes be asked to dinner, every year a summer departure to the country for a month but definitely free from work! . . . And perhaps even a little, a very little, baby? Will this never be permitted? Never? Darling, do you know what accosted me yesterday during a walk in the park – and without any exaggeration? A little child, three or four years old, in a beautiful dress with blond hair; it stared at me and suddenly I felt an overpowering urge to kidnap the child and dash off home with him. Oh darling, will I never have my own baby?

And at home we will never argue again, will we? It must be quiet and peaceful as it is with everyone else. Only you know what worries me, I feel already so old and am not in the least attractive. You will not have an attractive wife when you walk hand in hand with her through the park – we will keep well away from the Germans . . . Darling, if you will first settle the question of your citizenship, secondly your doctorate and thirdly live with me openly in our own room and work together with me, then we can want for nothing more! No couple on earth has so many facilities for happiness as you and I and if there is only some goodwill on our part we will be, must be, happy.

Empress Alexandra of Russia
1872–1918

Alexandra's mother was Princess Alice, the second daughter of Queen Victoria; her father was Prince Louis of the Grand Duchy of Hesse. Princess Alice was energetic and forward-thinking and a great philanthropist with a particular interest in the education and training of women. She died of diphtheria following a visit to a hospital when Alexandra was only six.

Alexandra and Nicholas, the Tsarevich of Russia, had fallen in love against the opposition both of Queen Victoria and of Nicholas's father, the Tsar. But with the Tsar in failing health, the objections were eventually overcome. He died on 1 November 1894; later that month, Nicholas and Alexandra were married and Alexandra became Tsarina. But life at the Russian court proved problematic. The people suspected her of being pro-German – which became an even more serious problem with the outbreak of the First World War; the nobility thought her insufficiently grand to have become empress; and her mother-in-law, the Dowager Empress, did everything she could to undermine her, including openly sneering at the fact that after ten years of marriage she had produced only daughters. Finally, in 1904, she gave birth to Alexei, the Tsarevich. Her joy and relief must have turned to anguish when she realized that he had inherited haemophilia, an often fatal condition at the time. The knowledge that it had been passed down from her side of the family – Queen Victoria was a carrier – must have made it even more difficult to bear.

In despair over the fragile health of her son, with doctors who were unable to offer any help, Alexandra turned to an array of healers, seers and mystics, the most notorious of whom was Rasputin, a kind of non-aligned monk of shady background and no credentials. Photographs show a greasy-haired, long-bearded middle-aged man striking a quasi-religious pose in the apparent belief that a mad, staring facial expression is the mark of a true mystic. Rasputin became, if possible, even more unpopular with both the people and the nobility than Alexandra herself, and was murdered by a gang of courtiers in 1916.

From some accounts of Alexandra's relationship with this charlatan, one might think she was single-handedly responsible for the Russian Revolution. But by 1917, the country was on its knees: famine was widespread, the mismanaged war dragged on, soldiers were opening fire on protestors and the Tsar – completely backed up by Alexandra, as can be seen below – refused to contemplate any kind of constitutional reform. After the February revolution Nicholas was forced to abdicate. He and his family were imprisoned by the Bolsheviks in various locations, and finally taken to a house at Ekaterinburg in the Urals. There, in the middle of the night of 16–17 July 1918, the entire family and three servants were taken by their guards from their sleeping quarters to the basement where, in a bloody chaos of bullets and bayonets, they were all killed.

To Tsar Nicholas II

Lovy dear, my telegrams can't be very warm, as they go through so many military hands – but you will read all my love and longing between the lines. Sweety, if in any way you do not feel quite the thing, you will be sure to call Feodorov, won't you – & have an eye on Fredericks.

My very most earnest prayers will follow you by day and night. I commend you into our Lord's safe keeping – may He guard, guide & lead you & bring you safe & sound back again.

I bless you & love you, as man has rarely been loved

before – & kiss every dearly beloved place & press you tenderly to my own heart.

For ever yr. Very own old
Wify

The Image will lie this night under my cushion before I give it to you with my fervent blessing.

To Tsar Nicholas II
Sent from Tsarskoje Selo, 4 December 1916

My Very Precious One,
Good-bye, sweet Lovy!

Its great pain to let you go – worse than ever after the hard times we have been living & fighting through. But God who is all love & mercy has let the things take a change for the better, – just a little more patience & deepest faith in the prayers & help of our Friend – then all will go well. I am fully convinced that great & beautiful times are coming for yr. Reign & Russia. Only keep up your spirits, let no talks or letters pull you down – let them pass by as something unclean & quickly to be forgotten.

Show to all, that you are the Master & your will shall be obeyed – the time of great indulgence & gentleness is over – now comes your reign of will & power, & they shall be made to bow down before you & listen to your orders & to work how & with whom you wish – obedience they must be taught, they do not know the meaning of that word, you have spoilt them by yr. kindness & all forgivingness.

Why do people hate me? Because they know I have a strong will & when am convinced of a thing being right (when besides blessed by *Gregory*), do not change my mind & that they can't bear. But its the bad ones.

Remember Mr Phillips words when he gave me the image with the bell. As you were so kind, trusting & gentle, I was to be yr. bell, those that came with wrong intentions wld. not be able to approach me & I wld. warn you. Those who are afraid of me, don't look me in the eyes or are up to some wrong, never like me. – Look at the black ones – then Orlov & Drenteln – Witte – *Kokovtzev* – *Trepov*, I feel it too – *Makarov* – *Kaufmann* – *Sofia Ivanovna* – *Mary* – *Sandra* Oblensky, etc., but those who are good & devoted to you honestly & purely – love me, – look at the simple people & military. The good & bad clergy its all so clear & therefore no more hurts me as when I was younger. Only when one allows oneself to write you or me nasty impertinent letters – you must punish.

Ania told me about *Balaschov* (the man I always disliked). I understood why you came so awfully late to bed & why I had such pain & anxiety writing. Please, Lovy, tell Frederiks to write him a strong *reprimand* (he & *Nicolai Mikhailovitch* & Vass make one in the club – he has such a high court-rank & dares to write, unasked. And its not the first time – in bygone days I remember he did so too. Tear up the letter, but have him firmly reprimanded – tell *Voyeikov* to remind the old man – such a smack to a conceited member of the Council of the Empire will be very useful.

We cannot now be trampled upon. Firmness above all! – Now you have made *Trepov's* son A.D.C. you can insist yet more on his working with *Protopopov*, he must prove his gratitude. – Remember to forbid *Gurko* speaking & mixing himself into politics – it ruined *Nikolasha* & Alexeiev, – the latter God sent this illness clearly to save you fr. a man who was losing his way & doing harm by listening to bad letters & people, instead of listening to yr. orders about the war & being obstinate. And one has set him against me – proof – what he said to old Ivanov. –

But soon all this things will blow over, its getting clearer & the weather too, which is a good sign, remember.

And our dear Friend is praying so hard for you – a man of God's near one gives the strength, faith & hope one needs so sorely. And others cannot understand this great calm of yours & therefore think you don't understand & try to ennervate, frighten & prick at you. But they will soon tire of it.

Should Mother dear write, remember the Michels are behind her. – Don't heed & take to heart – thank God, she is not here, but kind people find means of writing & doing harm. All is turning to the good – our Friends dreams mean so much. Sweety, go to the *Moghilev* Virgin & find peace and strength there – look in after tea, before you receive, take Baby with you, quietly – its so calm there – & you can place yr. candels. Let the people see you are a christian Sovereign & don't be shy – even such an example will help others. –

How will the lonely nights be? I cannot imagine it. The

consolation to hold you tightly clasped in my arms – it lulled the pain of soul & heart & I tried to put all my endless love, prayers & faith & strength into my caresses. So inexpressibly dear you are to me, husband of my heart. God bless you & my Baby treasure – I cover you with kisses; when sad, go to Baby's room & sit a bit quietly there with his nice people. Kiss the beloved child & you will feel warmed & calm. All my love I pour out to you, Sun of my life. –

Sleep well, heart & soul with you, my prayers around you – God & the holy Virgin will never forsake you –

Ever your very, very,

Own

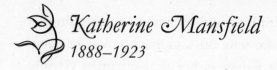

Katherine Mansfield
1888–1923

Katherine Mansfield was born Kathleen Beauchamp in Wellington, New Zealand, to parents of English descent. Her father was a successful self-made industrialist, and he and his wife were financially and socially ambitious. Kathleen was their third daughter; two more were followed by a son, Leslie.

In 1903 Katherine (she changed her name around this time) and her two older sisters were sent to Europe to be 'finished'; they attended a progressive school in London, where Katherine began a lifelong friendship with another pupil, Ida Baker, edited the school magazine and took holidays in Paris and Brussels. She returned to New Zealand in 1906, but agitated strongly to be allowed to go back to London. After she embarked on an affair with a young woman painter, her parents relented, and she left New Zealand for the last time in 1908.

The year following Katherine's arrival in London was chaotic, and had repercussions for the rest of her life. Having fallen in love with a fellow expatriate, a musician named Garnet Trowell, she joined a touring opera company (she was an accomplished cellist) in order to be with him, and became pregnant. On discovering this, she took off and married a respectable singing teacher ten years her senior named George Bowden. She fled immediately after the ceremony to take refuge with her friend Ida. Her mother came halfway around the world to investigate, and – having delivered a lecture to Ida's family on the dangers of lesbianism – whipped her off to a spa in Germany, where Katherine had a miscarriage. Mrs Beauchamp unceremoniously abandoned her there and returned to Wellington, where she promptly cut her daughter out of her will.

Katherine was able to return to London only after Ida paid her fare back from Germany. In the meantime, she had taken up with a Pole named Floryan Sobienowski, whom she was planning to marry in Paris. This plan seems to have been shelved when Katherine became seriously ill with untreated gonorrhoea, which left her requiring surgery and ended her chances of ever having a child.

One fruitful aspect of Katherine's enforced stay at the spa was a collection of stories, *In a German Pension*, which attracted some favourable attention when it was published in 1911, and led to her meeting John Middleton Murry, the editor of an avant-garde magazine named *Rhythm*. The two set up house together, after a fashion, and the next four years were spent flitting between London and Paris, dodging creditors, putting out the magazine and striking up friendships with a circle of writers and artists that included D. H. Lawrence and his lover, later wife, Frieda Weekley. Katherine did not produce any work during this time, and in 1915 left on her own for Paris, where she embarked on an affair with a French writer and began work on probably her most famous story, 'Prelude'. She returned to Murry in May. That October her brother Leslie, who had joined the army and was serving in France, was killed; the grieving Katherine insisted on travelling through the war-ravaged country, where Murry joined her shortly afterwards. A period of something approaching tranquillity and productive work in the south of France came to an end when the Lawrences summoned their friends to Zennor in Cornwall to take part in an experiment in communal living, which, somewhat predictably given the temperaments involved, lasted a matter of weeks.

Katherine was diagnosed with tuberculosis early in 1918 and went to France, accompanied by Ida, for treatment. She returned that March because her divorce from Bowden had finally come through and she and Murry were free to marry, which they did on 3 May. But the remaining years of Katherine's life were a blur of travel between London, France and Switzerland, as she attempted to stay one step ahead of the disease which she knew was killing her. She tried many treatments, some undeniably quackish, some straightforwardly harmful, and finally came to rest at an establishment at Fontainebleau, outside Paris, run by a Greek-Armenian guru. On 9 January 1923, Murry was permitted to visit her there; she died the same evening.

Murry became the guardian of her manuscripts, and for the twenty years after her death devoted himself to editing and publishing the letters, journals, stories and poems she had left behind, securing her reputation as one of the most influential writers of the early twentieth century (and not doing badly out of the proceeds, it must be said; Ida Baker, after years of devoted friendship, received nothing).

The first three letters below date from Katherine's stay in Paris after she began an affair with a French writer. Seen in that context, they are fascinating in their apparent neediness – presumably Katherine had realized by then that she wanted to return home. The final letter here is not a love letter, but demonstrates her method for dealing with rivals for her husband's affections. Even now, its icy condescension is quite terrifying.

To John Middleton Murry
Sent from Paris, 19 March 1915

Very strange is my love for you tonight. Don't have it psycho-analysed. I saw you suddenly lying in a hot bath, blinking up at me – your charming beautiful body half under the water. I sat on the edge of the bath in my vest waiting to come in. Everything in the room was wet with steam and it was night-time and you were rather languid. 'Tig, chuck over that sponge.' No, I'll *not* think of you like that. I'll shut my teeth and not listen to my heart. It begins to cry as if it were a child in an empty room and to beat on the door and say 'Jack – Jack – Jack and Tig.' I'll be better when I've had a letter.

Ah, my God, how can I love him like this! Do I love you so much more than you love me or do you too . . . feel like this?

TIG

Saturday morning. Just off to see if there are any letters. I'm all right, dearest.

To John Middleton Murry, 26 March 1915

Dearest darling,
I'm in such a state of worry and suspense that I can't write to you tonight or send you anything. When I came back from the fruitless search for letters the concierge began a long story about an Alsatian in the house who had received

yesterday a four-page letter for the name of Bowden.*
'Another came today,' said she, 'I gave it back to the postman.' I literally screamed. I have *written* this name for her
and she'd utterly forgotten it, thinking of me only as Mansfield. Since then I've simply rushed from post-office to
post-office. The Alsatian is out. I'm waiting for her and the
postman now. My heart dies in my breast with terror at the
thought of a letter of yours being lost. I simply don't exist.
I suppose I exaggerate – but I'd plunge into the Seine – or
lie on a railway line – rather than lose a letter. You know,
bogey, my heart is simply crying all the time and I am frightened, desolate, useless for anything.

Oh, my precious – my beloved little Jag, forgive Tig such
a silly scrawl.

But life ought not to do such things to you and me. I
could *kill* the concierge – yes, with pleasure. 'Une lettre
d'Angleterre dans un couvert bleu.'

Courage! But at this moment I am simply running as fast
as I can and crying my loudest into your arms.

I will write you properly tomorrow. This is just to say that
I love you and that you are the breath of life to me.

Tig

* Katherine's married name

To John Middleton Murry, 28 March 1915

Jack, I shan't hide what I feel today. I woke up with you in my breast and on my lips. Jack, I love you terribly today. The whole world is gone. There is only you. I walk about, dress, eat, write – but all the time I am *breathing* you. Time and again I have been on the point of telegraphing you that I am coming home as soon as Kay sends my money. It is still possible that I shall.

> *Jack, Jack, I want to come back,*
> *And to hear the little ducks go*
> *Quack! Quack! Quack!*

Life is too short for our love even though we stayed together every moment of all the years. I cannot think of you – our life – our darling life – you, my treasure – everything about you.

No, no, no. Take me quickly into your arms. Tig is a tired girl and she is crying. I want you, I want you. Without you life is nothing.

Your woman

Tig

My darling

Do not imagine, because you find these lines in your private book that I have been trespassing. You know I have not – and where else shall I leave a love letter? For I long to write you a love letter tonight. You are all about me – I seem to breathe you – hear you – feel you in me and of me – What am I doing here? You are away – I have seen you in the train, at the station, driving up, sitting in the lamplight talking, greeting people – washing your hands – And I am here – in your tent – sitting at your table. There are some wallflower petals on the table and a dead match, a blue pencil and a *Magdeburgische Zeitung*. I am just as much at home as they.

When dusk came – flowing up the silent garden – lapping against the blind windows – my first & last terror started up – I was making some coffee in the kitchen. It was so violent, so dreadful I put down the coffee-pot – and simply ran away – ran out of the studio and up the street with my bag under one arm and a block of writing paper and a pen under the other. I felt that if I could get here & find Mrs [illegible] I should be 'safe' – I found her and I lighted your gas, wound up your clock – drew your curtains – & embraced your black overcoat before I sat down – frightened no longer. Do not be angry with me, Bogey – ca a ete plus fort que moi . . . That is why I am here.

When you came to tea this afternoon you took a brioche broke it in half & padded the inside doughy bit with two fingers. You always do that with a bun or a roll or a piece of bread – It is your way – your head a little on one side the while . . .

When you opened your suitcase I saw your old feltie and a French book and a comb all higgledy piggledy – 'Tig. I've only got 3 handkerchiefs' – Why should that memory be so sweet to me? . . .

Last night, there was a moment before you got into bed. You stood, quite naked, bending forward a little – talking. It was only for an instant. I saw you – I loved you so – loved your body with such tenderness – Ah my dear – And I am not thinking now of 'passion'. No, of that other thing that makes me feel that every inch of you is so precious to me. Your soft shoulders – your creamy warm skin, your ears, cold like shells are cold – your long legs and your feet that I love to clasp with my feet – the feeling of your belly – & your thin young back – Just below that bone that sticks out at the back of your neck you have a little mole. It is partly because we are young that I feel this tenderness – I love your youth – I could not bear that it should be touched even by a cold wind if I were the Lord.

We two, you know have everything before us, and we shall do very great things – I have perfect faith in us – and so perfect is my love for you that I am, as it were, still, silent to my very soul. I want nobody but you for my

lover and my friend and to nobody but you shall I be
faithful.

I am yours for ever.

Tig

To John Middleton Murry, Sunday night, 27 January 1918

My love and my darling,
It is ten minutes past eight. I must tell you how much I love
you at ten minutes past eight on a Sunday evening, January
27th 1918.

I have been indoors all day (except for posting your letter) and I feel greatly rested. Juliette has come back from a
new excursion into the country, with blue irises – do you
remember how beautifully they grew in that little house
with the trellis tower round by the rocks? – and all sorts and
kinds of sweet-smelling jonquils . . . The room is very
warm. I have a handful of fire, and the few little flames
dance on the log and can't make up their minds to attack it
. . . There goes a train. Now it is quiet again except for my
watch. I look at the minute hand and think what a spectacle
I shall make of myself when I am really coming home to
you. How I shall sit in the railway carriage, and put the old
watch in my lap and pretend to cover it with a book – but
not read or see, but just whip it up with my longing gaze,
and simply make it go faster.

My love for you tonight is so deep and tender that it seems
to be outside myself as well. I am fast shut up like a little lake

in the embrace of some big mountains, you would see me down below, deep and shining – and quite fathomless, my dear. You might drop your heart into me and you'd never hear it touch bottom. I love you – I love you – Goodnight.

Oh, Bogey, what it is to love like this!

To Princess Bibesco (née Elizabeth Asquith, 1897–1945, daughter of Herbert Asquith and Margot Tennant, married to a Romanian diplomat twenty-two years her senior), 24 March 1921

Dear Princess Bibesco,
I am afraid you must stop writing these little love letters to my husband while he and I live together. It is one of the things which is not done in our world.

You are very young. Won't you ask your husband to explain to you the impossibility of such a situation.

Please do not make me have to write to you again. I do not like scolding people and I simply hate having to teach them manners.

Yours sincerely,
Katherine Mansfield

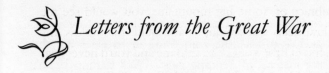

Letters from the Great War

The First World War raged from 1914 to 1918, and was the first truly global war in history, with fronts in Europe, the Middle East, Africa and Asia. The casualty figures are devastating: one in three British families had a loved one killed, wounded or taken prisoner. The letters below from a woman in Walthamstow to her soldier husband, remarkable for their brightness and bravery, give a tiny insight into what life was like for those left behind.

Walthamstow E17, 17 September 1916

My Dearest one and only,

Oh for the sight of your dear face, I feel it more everyday, it seems years since you were here and took dear Baby and I in your arms and when I look out and see the pouring rain my heart feels fit to break to think of you in the cold dismal tent, while I am at home with a nice fire. Oh dear it does seem terrible to me and you've done nothing to deserve it. Sunday seems the same as every day but worse today it's the 17th dear. Well dear matey I have sent this parcel and hope you will like them, they are plain this time and also kerchieves and another undervest, which in unfolding be careful, as I've put a little something in to celebrate the anniversery instead of sending cigs – Well darling I can't think of any more new just now but let me know if anything you are needing, by the way would you like a couple of pig's bladders to fill your breeches out, they'd make fine cushions as well, that's the worst of these cheap bums. Heaps of love and kisses from your dear little Baby and everloving devoted wifie

25 June 1917

My Own dear Hubby,
Your dear letter of Sat. just received – Well darling mine I have just a little news to tell you which I'm sure you will regret to hear. Poor Harry Saville has gone under, news have just come through that he was shot on the 10th & died of his wounds on the 15th & they never had notice he was wounded even, so it was a terrible shock to them, poor Mrs S. is properly knocked over & Mrs Styles son lays at Bournemouth badly wounded from France. Oh darling it seems so terrible if only it would end and send you back to me. I should know you were safe, it seems ages & ages since your dear face was before me & when one hears bad news it makes you feels so downhearted – Excuse this scrawl as I've got Baby in my arms asleep and it's rather difficult – Cheer up sweetheart all my dearest love to you darling & heaps of kisses from your dear little treasure who says

daddy's gone to fight the naughty shermans & she wont love em. Your everloving everlonging & devoted to you wife and Babs

5 November 1917

My own dearest one,

At last thank God I have heard from you, from Durban dated Sept 19 & 20 & one posted at sea all 3 arrived together on 30 october & silk hanky as well, after long weary months of waiting my patients were rewarded & thanks awfully darling it was so sweet of you, to see your dear writing once more was like a hidden treasure. What an experience for you dearest & what a lot you will have to tell dear babby & I when you return to us again, & how many an evening we shall sit in the dear firelight listening to all your travels. What a time that will be dear, one can hardly realise it, if only it was for some other purpose, one could be so very much happier, but there dear that's the way of this wicked war, so I must buck up for your dear sake, & we will make up for all this when you come back to us which I pray please God will not be much longer now as we are all fed up with it – And your sweet little daughter joins me with all our dearest, best & devoted love to you dear & lots of loving kisses, & hope you will come safely home to us soon.

The following sources were invaluable:

Love in Letters Illustrated in the Correspondence of Eminent Persons with Biographical Sketches of the Writers by Allan Grant, G. W. Carleton & Co., New York 1867

Love Letters of Famous Men and Women, J. T. Merydew (ed.), Remington & Co., London 1888

Love Affairs of Famous Men & Women, Henri Pène du Bois (ed.), Gibbings & Company, London 1900

The Letters of Robert Browning and Elizabeth Barrett Browning, Smith, Elder & Co., London, 1900

Love Letters of Famous People, Freeman Bunting (ed.), Gay and Bird, London, 1907

Letters of Love, Arthur L. Humphreys, London 1911

Love Letters of Great Men and Women, C. H. Charles (ed.), Stanley Paul & Co, London, 1924

The Love Letters of Robert Burns and Clarinda, Donny O'Rourke (ed.), based on 1843 edition, edited by W. C. M'Lehose

Mark Twain's Letters, edited and with a commentary by Albert Bigelow Paine, Harper & Brothers Publishers, New York, 1917

Love Letters, Antonia Fraser (ed.), Weidenfeld & Nicolson, London, 1976

Love Letters, Peter Washington (ed.), Everyman's Library, 1996

Dispatches from the Heart: Love Letters from the Front Line, Jamie Ambrose (ed.), Little Books Ltd, London, 2005

Love Letters: An Anthology from the British Isles, 975–1944, James Turner (ed.), Cassell & Company Ltd, London, 1970

The Virago Book of Love Letters, Jill Dawson (ed.), Virago Press Ltd, London, 1994

The Virago Book of Women and the Great War, Joyce Marlow (ed.), Virago Press Ltd., London, 1998

The Massachusetts Historical Society online archive, www.masshist.org

Project Gutenberg, www.gutenberg.org

Acknowledgements

Thanks to JG for the idea, JB for commissioning it, RM for letting him, FC, KT, WD and IA for making it look lovely, and to all my friends at Pan Macmillan. Thanks to LG and UM and my friends at Little Brown. Thanks to the staff at the British Library. Thanks to my family, immediate and extended, great men and women all. And thanks above all to DP, runner of support services, van man supreme, best beloved.